Dear Dave,
To add e
more fun
road trip Lu: ✱
Li'z
✱ma-

FLATTENED FAUNA

A FIELD GUIDE TO COMMON ANIMALS OF ROADS, STREETS, AND HIGHWAYS

— REVISED —

The definitive guide for the millions of people who seldom see a wild animal that has not been flattened by the dozens of vehicles ahead of them, and baked by the sun to an indistinct fur-, scale-, or feather-covered patty.

Roger M. Knutson

TEN SPEED PRESS
Berkeley | Toronto

Ten Speed Press
P.O. Box 7123
Berkeley, California 94707
www.tenspeed.com

Distributed in Australia by Simon and Schuster Australia, in
Canada by Ten Speed Press Canada, in New Zealand by Southern
Publishers Group, in South Africa by Real Books, and in the United
Kingdom and Europe by Publishers Group UK.

Cover and text design by Chloe Rawlins
Cover photography: Will & Deni McIntyre / Getty Images

Library of Congress Cataloging-in-Publication Data on file
with the publisher.

Knutson, Roger M., 1933-
        Flattened fauna.
        Bibliography: p. 83
        Includes index.
        1. Roadside fauna-United States-Identification.
2. Urban fauna-United States-Identification.
1. Title
QL.155.K58   1987   596.097386-23105

ISBN-13: 978-1-58008-755-1
ISBN-10: 1-58008-755-8

Printed in the United States of America
1 2 3 4 5 6 7 8 9 10 — 10 09 08 07 06

Contents

International Flat Fauna Reporting Form

(may be duplicated as necessary)

Mail completed form to:

Headquarters, International Simmons Society
408 Burns Street
Charlevoix, MI 49720-1025

Date

Country

Province or State

Organism name (local)

(Latin)

Brief description of roadside vegetation (e.g., forest type, savanna, vegetation density, water sources nearby, etc.)

Name and address of informant:

Additional information:

chapter 1

Introduction

This is a book about the animals that, like the Wicked Witch of the East in *The Wizard of Oz*, are not just merely dead but really most sincerely dead. These are animals in which even flies have lost interest.

A guide to live animals would work well as a guide to the merely dead, since the descriptions in most guides to live animals are based on dead, stuffed animals in museums. However, a guide to the animals of the road has specific reasons for being: in becoming part of the road fauna celebrated in this book, an animal loses not only its life but also its third dimension. And though it has lost most of its mass and much of its normal shape, the creature is not bereft of its interest to naturalists. It is not on the road by accident, although it certainly did not plan its abrupt arrival. The road fauna is made up of creatures who are victims of their own habits—feeding habits, reproductive habits and aggressive or agonistic behavior habits. All these habits enhance survival in the creature's usual environment, but produce serious dismemberment, and even enroadment, on the highway. Why an animal is on the road and what it was doing there a few hours or days earlier are recorded in its flat remains as surely as the history of a tree is recorded in its annual rings.

Dead and flattened animals on the road are a part of the common experience of everyone who lives where there are roads, from the family on a drive in the country to the daily commuter traveling the same route 250 days each year. Or from the bike rider on the quiet park road to the professional truck-driver who spends hundreds of hours per month on major highways.

Much of our usual appreciation of an animal—in any condition—depends on our ability to identify and name it. For flattened fauna, however, that can be a problem. Most of these animals have been pressed to the road for several days and may have assumed unrecognizable shapes. This book is devoted to making the experience of seeing dead animals on the road meaningful, even enjoyable. With *Flattened Fauna* in hand, a Sunday drive can become a safari into a new habitat populated with animals unlike those you have seen before. This guide is meant to answer the oft-asked question, "That wasn't a dog or cat—what was it?"[1]

We all love to look at animals. But for every mile we walk in the natural world, looking for animals, we may drive 200 miles. Much of the driving is done, ironically, in an effort to get to a zoo, park, or natural area where we can observe animals. For every live animal we may observe, we are likely to see anywhere from five to twenty-five animals plastered to the pavement. The commonly available guides to wildlife take no account of this fact. The usual picture guides and handbooks of wildlife suggest that we are more likely to see a chipmunk nibbling a nut on the end of a log than lying in the middle of the road as a patch of striped brown fur; that we more often see a rabbit bounding through our back yard than on the turnpike, with its three strangely angled legs, one ear, and white powder-puff of a tail. Those (up to now) nondescript spots and blotches of fur, feathers, and scales are the wildlife we see most often, yet nowhere has there been a guide to their identification. *Flattened Fauna* is meant to fill that gap and encourage our appreciation of that part of the natural world found on any nation's highway surfaces.

---

[1] No domestic animals are included in this book because their habits are governed by their responses to people rather than to their habitat. The death of a pet may well be a tragedy, the death on the highway of a squirrel can be both interesting and informative.

Various historical estimates place the density of flattened animals at from 0.429 to 4.10 animals per mile of prime highway habitat.[2] This means that a trip of 1000 miles (1600 kilometers) could be the occasion for seeing, identifying, and even enjoying anywhere from 400 to 4000 animals.

Of course numbers will vary with season and location, but the adventure of seeing and identifying this truly stationary wildlife in large numbers can now be available to anyone who travels roads and byways. The flattened fauna of our highways—road fauna—allows everyone to discover and describe animals in a habitat that is abundantly available. A cross-country family trip, once a test of parental patience and ingenuity, can now be nearly as exciting as a visit to the Serengeti Plain. The logbook of a dead-animal aficionado in California, on one 480-mile trip in the spring of 1984, revealed a total of nine reptiles, 58 birds, and 161 mammals. A late summer vacation along the highways of almost any country will provide an even larger number of sightings. The current world record for one day's observation, dating back to 1933 (when rabbits may have been less highway savvy) is 598 rabbits on 50 miles of two-lane asphalt road near Boise, Idaho. That record will not be broken on any busy four-lane highway. High speed and heavy traffic are not compatible with a high density of flat animals. Some animals are smart enough to stay off a road frequented by large numbers of fast-moving vehicles.

The Road as Habitat

Compared to places where animals live, the road is an unusual habitat. Most animal habitats (forests, marshes, prairies, and sand dunes) have been part of the natural world for millions of years. The creatures that live in those places have developed more or less precise adaptations to their particular

---

[2] See H. Elliot McClure. 1951. An analysis of animal victims on Nebraska's highways. *Journal of Wildlife Management* 15:410–420.

niches. The road fauna, by contrast, occupy a habitat that is almost unique to the twentieth century. An unwary prairie dog (*Cynomys ludivicianus*) may have worked its way into the soil of the Oregon Trail under the wheels of a nineteenth-century Conestoga wagon. A reliable 1897 report[3] from North Dakota gives evidence of at least one large snapping turtle (*Chelydra serpentina*) flattened under the steel-rimmed wheels of several loaded wagons. Even more rarely, a European brown hare (*Lepus capensis*) may have been unable to avoid an onrushing Roman chariot. But until the twentieth century, the roads and vehicles that have been the major molders of road fauna were so rare that they scarcely concerned biologists interested in the relationships of animal to habitat. Fast cars and hard-surfaced roads have produced the entire flattened fauna described here in less than an eye-blink of evolutionary time.

How have animals responded to this modern habitat? Will they evolve appropriate adaptations to the road? Evolutionary theory tells us that the organisms of any recently developed habitat will show characteristics of instability and local variation. (As a new habitat is invaded by any species, the prior restraints on its reproduction and variation relax, usually resulting in a multitude of new forms.) The reproductive potential of the flattened fauna is, of course, very low, but variation in form is certainly characteristic. While the road fauna does show a multitude of unique, two dimensional forms, it has existed for less than 100 years—insufficient time for adaptations or discernable evolutionary development. It is most probably the case that, like the Shakers, the road fauna depends completely on recruitment rather than reproduction for its "survival," and cannot be expected to show evolutionary changes no matter how much time has passed.

Yoram Yom-Tov's 1997 paper on "The Evolution of Two-dimensional Vertebrates," from the *Israel Journal of Zoology*,

---

[3] The Snapping Turtle report is a personal communication from John Tjostem, a colleague, who was citing his grandmother's diary.

offers an alternative point of view. He suggests that the evolution of the road fauna is proceeding at an accelerated pace,
going through a period of extremely rapid change. This sug-
gestion requires, however, that the new organisms found on
the road are in fact unique species, derived from earlier forms.
Taxonomists will always disagree on strict classification, and
I cannot support the ideas that all the road forms are new
species: varieties, maybe, but not new species. To quote, more
or less accurately, our President, "I'm a lumper, not a splitter."

If the road habitat and its major selective pressure—fast-
moving vehicles—were to persist, a field guide written a few
thousand years hence might show the beginnings of characteristics specifically related to long-term survival on the road.
When roads have been a dominant feature of the natural
environment for many centuries, we might expect turtles
with very sturdy, nearly flat shells to emerge by the normal
processes of natural selection. Animals that tunnel under
roads would certainly be at some advantage as road habitat
becomes more and more abundant; so would those organisms
that have managed some cooperative co-evolution with birds
that could ferry them across highways. Any dramatic increase
in animal speed would not be very useful and is not expected.

Precise evolutionary adaptations have always been difficult to forecast, although the history of life on earth suggests
that, given enough time, most habitats—even the most
hazardous—develop their own distinctive assemblage of
animals. Indeed, that development may have already begun.
Victor B. Sheffer's book, *Spires of Form, Glimpses of Evolution*,
quotes a friend in England who believes that "hedgehogs
have learned genetically, within our century to run from
approaching automobiles instead of curling up in the defen-
sive posture of their pre-auto ancestors." If English hedgehogs
can do it, we should expect animals anywhere on earth to
follow suit. By contrast, Professor Yom-Tov writes that hedgehogs are more likely to develop two-dimensionality than any
other mammal.

What follows, then, is a systematic look at a very recently developed habitat and its unusual animal inhabitants: squashed squirrels, flat flickers, battered badgers, mangled marmots, and retrorse rabbits.

History and Future of the Road Fauna

At a time when the total world fauna is surely shrinking in both absolute numbers and species complexity, the road fauna is clearly increasing. Before 1900 in the United States, its presence was recorded by only the most fragmentary references to the occasional horse-stomped snake. With the development in the twentieth century of a much elongated road network and dramatically increased traffic speed, the flattened fauna has increased in both species and total numbers. There is little published research before 1930, but in 1938 Thomas G. Scott measured a density of 0.429 organisms per mile and estimated that a total of 39.1462 animals entered the flattened fauna annually per mile of Iowa highway.[4] Mr. Scott recorded fifty-seven different species, nearly half of them birds. In his 1938 classic, *Feathers and Fur on the Turnpike*,[5] New Englander James Simmons documented species numbers as great as those from Iowa. By 1944, in a thorough examination of the Nebraska road fauna based on 77,000 miles of travel, H. Elliott McClure[6] was able to find 101 species and a total of 6,723 specimens. (Again, half the species were birds.) Obviously the road fauna was expanding rapidly, with forty-four additional species in only six years. This was happening, moreover, even with lowered (35 mph) speed limits imposed to save gasoline during World War II.

---

[4] Scott, Thomas G. 1938. Wildlife mortality on Iowa's highways. *American Midland Naturalist* 20:527–539.

[5] Simmons, James R. 1983. *Feathers and fur on the turnpike*. Boston: Christopher Publishing House.

[6] McClure, H. Elliott. 1951. An analysis of animal victims on Nebraska's highways. *Journal of Wildlife Management* 15:410–420.

Extrapolating this six-year increase over the decades from 1945 to the present, 2005 may reveal well over 500 species in the flattened fauna of North America—a truly robust phenomenon. Current research to verify these predictions is incomplete.

Information from outside North America is even more sparse. China and India are not only adding people to the world, they are adding roads and vehicles. (See Chapter 2 for an international perspective.) Worldwide public attention to the growth of the road fauna may be the most important environmental issue of the twenty-first century. Even as we face large-scale animal extinction over much of the world, the flattened fauna grows. It deserves international attention.

In order to expand our understanding of the world's road animals, we need a society modeled after the most successful educational and information-gathering organization in zoological history: the Audubon Society. If the flattened fauna is to have a patron saint, we could do no better than J. R. Simmons, whose immortal and nearly unavailable work, *Feathers and Fur on the Turnpike*, brought to the attention of all who read it vital information about the road fauna of New England.

An International Simmons Society has been established with headquarters at 408 Burns Street in Charlevoix, Michigan. There have been semi-active chapters of the society in Boulder, Colorado, and in Leeds, England. Interest in the organization has been expressed in Australia and in Germany. A network of dead animal fans is growing, even as the world's network of roads is expanding.

The most important early function of the Society has been routine semi-annual counts of road victims. The Labor Day count and Memorial Day count coincide with the most abundant presence of road animals in temperate climates, and the highest traffic totals. Any pattern of seasonal distribution in tropical regions is yet to be discerned. Documentation of changes in the number of individuals and species will serve to alert the lovers of dead things to the increases or decreases of some favorite species in the flattened fauna—information that is now recorded only sporadically and compiled only by the Simmons Society. Active members of the society are expected to maintain an up-to-date death list, which also helps to document any increase or decrease in species number. (See end pages for suggested format.)

The Seasonal Nature of the Road Fauna

Even the casual North American observer is aware that the road fauna is more abundant in some seasons than others. For a few species such as toads and frogs, migration for spring breeding produces that seasonal flurry of inactivity on the road. For most mammals and birds, however, the largest number of new specimens piles up in mid- to late summer. Though this peak might appear to be only the product of hordes of summer vacationers and busy weekend trippers, the truth is more biological. The proliferation of road fauna in July and August is a direct result of the abundance of animals living near the road at that time. Most of the surplus consists of young, naïve creatures—those with only the most limited experience of the road and its hazards. McClure's study of the road fauna in Nebraska revealed that sparrows flattened in July constituted 63 percent of the total flattened sparrows for the whole year. Young sparrows are most numerous in July. Thirty-one percent of all the red-headed woodpeckers found for the whole year were found in August, just when the young are beginning to fly and feed for themselves. And those young woodpeckers seek out food in the drifts of dead insects found along any highway.

For beginning temperate zone students of the road fauna, late summer will certainly be the best time to initiate their study. Anyone wishing to specialize in reptiles might well reserve time during September and October, as nights cool and the road is warm (see snakes, page 27). The pursuit of flattened forms of nearly all birds and mammals will be most productive in July and August.

In winter, the road fauna is seriously depleted in those places where many creatures have either migrated to warmer climates or are in hibernation. In colder climates, the general level of inactivity reduces absolute numbers, but the preservation effect of cold may compensate by retaining specimens on the road for longer periods. The only exceptions to this bleak winter picture of life without flattened animals on the road are some of the winter-active flocking birds, which will seek sand, salt, or grain along the roadsides. Sometimes dozens of individuals of the same species are found within a few hundred yards of one another—an abundance of flat birds seldom rivaled in quantity even during the most active summer seasons.

Mimicry and Protective Coloration in the Road Fauna

In pursuit of species survival, natural selection has produced many animals that resemble inanimate parts of their habitat. There are caterpillars that, at rest, look exactly like dead twigs, tigers whose stripes disappear in the sun-shadowed pattern of bamboo stalks, and insects that look like leaves, thorns, or flowers. We may question whether such mimicry exists among the animals on the road. For most of the flattened fauna, the analysis of mimicry is difficult at best, since neither the mimic nor the object of mimicry will blow its cover by moving. Whether the flattened sod clump mimics the flattened porcupine or vice versa is a moot point for the student of road animals, interesting thought it may be for the evolutionary biology (see Yoram Yom-Tov, "The Evolution of Two-dimensional Vertebrates"). The issue for the road naturalist is what non-animal objects on the road look like animals, and how we can tell them from one another.

The most extensive professional treatment of mimicry on the road to date appeared in the October 3, 1983 *New Yorker*. However, the author treated only the limited set of mimics represented by pieces of rubber tires that are so common along major highways. For those particular residents of the road he coined the word "recaptoids," and included among the animals only the "curving reptile," the "modified tarantula," and a "spectacular spiny crustacean." A spiny crustacean seems unlikely to appear on most roads, although I do have in my file of flat creatures a fine, two-dimensional sea star found on the Oregon Coast Highway. The recaptoid mimics are of limited interest in this guide. Only the curving reptile is likely to be among the common road fauna, and a genuinely flattened recaptoid is extremely rare. Most curl significantly above the road surface and are immediately distinguishable from any properly flattened animal, none of which retains any residual capacity to rise from the road. Although it is true that the wing of an occasional bird or the tail of a squirrel will lift and flap in the slipstream of large trucks, only totally black birds and black squirrels could be confused with any recaptoid.

Since exhaust systems parts are common along any road, an inexpensive short muffler, properly flattened, may at first glance resemble an armadillo. Coloration and segmentation are important distinguishing features in this case (armadillos have segments, mufflers do not), and few mufflers, even after long road residence, develop the gentle curves and tapered tail characteristics of the days-old flat or nearly flat armadillo.

A rusted hubcap looks enough like a painted turtle to confuse even the longtime student of road artifacts. Evidence of feet or a tail is the only certain way to distinguish the turtle from its mimic.

A chuck of recently cut sod fallen from a flatbed truck during dry weather will follow almost the same pattern of flattening and spreading as an equivalent-sized mammal. The green sod will bleach to pale tan, and the whole thing will look much like a prairie dog (*Cynomys ludovicianus*), which fortunately is rare near newer subdivisions where the sod may be common. Or the sod may resemble an upside-down yellow-bellied marmot (*Marmota flaveventris*), which is uncommon outside the mountainous regions of western North America. Sod chunks are also a good deal more solid than even the sturdiest mammal. I don't usually encourage driving over a specimen to help with identification, but if you suspect that the pale tan lump is a sod chunk mimic, drive over it. Two loud thumps from the tires will help confirm your suspicions. Yoram Yom-Tov reports in his examination of flat creatures that driving over them causes no change in shape or size.

Both tree branches and pieces of tree bark can resemble flattened fauna. Long, thin branches are probably the road objects nearest in shape to a road snake. But branches are always more resilient than snakes and will fray at the edges over time. Snakes almost never fray before total disintegration, and usually remain firmly fixed to the road at all points. Bark fragments of the right size present more of a puzzle than branches. They can be almost any shape, and as frayed edges develop they can look like some of the longer-furred small- to medium-sized mammals. Redwood bark and red squirrels are often confused, as are darker colored barks and uniformly colored mammals like the Norway rat (*Rattus norvegicus*), or a yellow-bellied marmot right-side up. Careful reference to the silhouettes in the guide will help, but at highway speeds, some mimics will escape proper identification.

Many mammals and birds in their off-road habitat remain totally stationary as protective behavior. However, both road fauna and the mimics are more or less permanently immobile, even while exposed on the highway. Once the animal is firmly on the road, only the tips of birds wings and the tails of squirrels tend to move much.

Food on the Road

Most animal habitats provide plants for the resident herbivores. The road is a peculiar habitat in that it provides almost no growing plants for food. Plant food on the road (all imported) consists of seeds blown from passing grain transports, occasional bits of badly wilted lettuce from a discarded McDonald's carton, or a few potato chips from a littering child. Animal food for the carnivores is produced in abundance right on the road—from the flattened animals themselves. An ecologist's dictum states, "Everything is food for something," and this certainly applies on the road. Everything organic that finds its way onto the road is likely to be used as food by something else that finds its way onto the road. Road carrion is among the major reasons why flesh-eating mammals become part of the flattened fauna. Ground squirrels nibble on bats, opossums on ground squirrels, and skunks on opossums, providing a fine two-dimensional example of food chains and the balance of nature.

It is safe to say that many of the animals on the road are or were seriously addicted to fast food—fast food is almost the only kind you can get on the road. For most of us, the only serious hazard likely from fast food on the road is indigestion if we eat too fast. For potential road fauna, not eating fast enough may carry a more permanent penalty: becoming the next course.

chapter 2

The International Study of the Road Fauna

The original edition of this guide concerned itself only with the road fauna of North America. Interest in that book became worldwide, and correspondence with *Flattened Fauna* aficionados on all continents except Antarctica has continued to the present time. While the particular creatures involved may vary from place to place, the principles outlined in Chapter 1 apply universally. The road fauna will crop up, or rather lie down, anywhere in the world that has roads and traffic. Antarctica would appear to be the only continent excluded.

While interest in the road fauna is almost universal, or at least multinational, objective, scientific information about the number, frequency, and species of two-dimensional animals is sadly lacking for areas outside North America. Even Europe is poorly represented. What follows constitutes something close to the sum of direct information about non–North American road fauna.

Unpublished correspondence about flat animals from personal communications has begun to establish part of the international picture. A 1989 report from what was then extreme eastern Zaire included not just information, but that rarest of artifacts, an actual road specimen. Paul Pena, who was a Peace Corps volunteer in the area of Lake Kivu near the Rwandan border, provided the first African specimen on record. The animal, *Chamaeleo dilepsis*, the African flap-necked chameleon, which is in the live condition already somewhat flattened laterally was near perfect, down to the clockwise curl of its tail. Road chameleons show no color change under any circumstances, although from the written description of the location, this particular specimen did nearly match in color its immediate highway environment. More such specimens and descriptive locality information would be most valuable.

The other African report is a published work from Tanzania which concerns primarily baboon mortality on highways. Apparently even animals smart enough to function as substitute goatherds are susceptible to the hazards of the road. Africa will clearly provide a rich environment for the road fauna as highway networks expand.

The most complete professional examination of European road fauna comes from Ireland. Sleeman, Smiddy, and Sweeney published papers in the *Irish Naturalist Journal* during the late 1980s documenting stoat and other mammal fatalities. An additional paper on badgers (*Meles meles*) on the roads of Denmark (J. Aaris-Sorenson) from 1995 contributes additional European information. More up-to-date data seems to be lacking. Sometimes obscure professional journals are the best source of real information. So far as I am aware, nothing on the subject has ever appeared in the international journals *Nature* or *Science*.

Tropical America should be a rich field for measurement of highway impact. As roads spread into the tropical forests of the Americas, literally thousands of new animals and birds may become part of the developing international road fauna. David Campbell in his 2005 book *A Land of Ghosts*, details both the development and the demise of the Transamazon Highway in the far eastern portions of the Amazon. The highway was built and then disintegrated within 20 years, from 1970 to 1990. Campbell's interest was in the botany and the sociology of the area and he made no recorded observations of highway animal mortality, although the impact of the highway on indigenous people was dramatic and tragic.

A magnificent contribution to the tropical American road fauna has come from Julian Monge-Najera of the University of Costa Rica. Professor Monge-Najera's work might well serve as a model for other investigators. In examining more than 10,000 kilometers of Costa Rican highways, a large number of species never before a part of the road fauna were added. Traffic volume is low by contrast with most North American highways, and total density of animals was 0.027 specimens per mile if domestic dogs and cats were included and only 0.019 per mile for wild reptiles, birds, and mammals. This contrasts with a value of 0.429 animals per mile for 1938 Iowa roads (see T. G. Scott, 1938).

While there are few animals in common between North America and Costa Rica, the basic principles helping to define the road fauna apply. The behaviors of animals that are found most frequently on the road are consistent regardless of the particular species or geographic area involved. Central American porcupines and skunks are important elements in Costa Rica as are the North American porcupines and skunks. Opossums are found on the highways of Central America for the same reason they are found in Alabama, even though the species of opossum are different. That two-toed sloths, with their much reduced metabolic rate, could not make it across the road is no surprise, but the common presence of a small, arboreal anteater permanently on the highway cries out for further investigation of its habits.

Twenty species of mammals were found in Professor Monge-Najera's study, along with six species of birds, four of reptiles, and a single amphibian species. The much smaller number of total organisms found in Costa Rica is attributed to the lower traffic volume and slower speeds as compared with North American highways.

Australia should be a fine source of road fauna information. However, I am not aware of any published work from

Australian highways. Correspondence and other personal communications suggest that interest is high. Aussies commonly refer to "making smart kangaroos" (the smart kangaroos are those that either make it across the road or do not attempt the journey) or thinning the wallaby numbers, but critical quantitative work is up to now missing. Since Australia represents a remarkable array of climatic and geographic areas, such information would be of great value in interpreting the international implications of road flattening.

The best solution to the paucity of information on the international scene is not to wait for professional biologists to develop interest, but to begin immediately the collection of information from dedicated amateurs. A sample form is included on page iv of this volume that could be duplicated and used to forward information about the flattened fauna of all corners of the globe. The headquarters of the International Simmons Society will maintain the central data bank, and serve to coordinate this international effort.

How and Where to Study the Road Fauna in North America

Interstate highways are a good place to begin your examination of the road fauna. Most miles of travel occur on such roads, and vehicle speed is sufficient to maintain interest in the beginning student. These highways tend to be more uniform from one part of the country to another than do secondary roads, so there are likely to be fewer regional differences in the number and variety of animal inhabitants on the interstates. For the beginner, the number of potential identifications more than makes up for the reduced diversity. Highway speeds also reduce the probability of seeing and identifying the smaller members of the road fauna. On the fast road, look for the larger specimens. The most common road fauna mammals include skunks, raccoons, porcupines, and marmots. Birds disappear from high speed roads so rapidly that it is rare to find a good one on an interstate. But the brighter colored woodpeckers and an occasional herring gull in coastal regions will develop your ability to spot birds. This skill will become more valuable as you extend your study to less-traveled routes with their more varied offerings.

Surveys by both professionals and amateurs have shown that the most varied and numerous specimens of the road fauna are likely to be found on less busy highways. Infrequently traveled roads, even those without asphalt or concrete surfaces, are often the most productive place to look for that relatively rare specimen to add to your life (or properly, death) list. I well remember finding an almost perfectly flat specimen of the Least Weasel (*Mustela nivalis*), one of the world's smallest carnivores, in northern Iowa in the outside wheel track of a little used rural asphalt road that must have had total traffic of less than one car per hour.

The keys and descriptions in this guide are meant to be used at highway speeds. However, situations with less traffic allow you to briefly slow to 30 mph and examine the specimen in a more leisurely fashion.

Secondary roads bordering marshes or wetlands are probably the best places for seeing the widest and flattest variety of species. Roadside vegetation is often a critical part of the effective habitat of road fauna, especially for those species that do not live directly on the road or road edge. A variety of turtles, snakes, frogs, marsh birds, and muskrats are commonly part of the flattened fauna near a marsh. Any marsh-edged road in late summer will be the best possible place to rapidly expand your "death" list.

Lakeside roads are less interesting than those near marshes, but an occasional gravity-stricken gull may make up for the lack of more familiar flat birds. Fish are so rare among the road fauna that I hesitate to mention them at all, but if you seek the thrill of that one rare, flat, finny specimen, you might spend some time on lake roads. The June-July 2005 issue of *National Wildlife Magazine* has a remarkable photograph of a large spawning salmon crossing the center-line of a partially flooded roadway in Oregon, and I have photo-graphic proof of a medium-sized guppy, flat as a sheet of paper, found on a small town street in northern Michigan.

Lonely roads with forest on one side and open fields or meadows on the other are prime locations for seeking out the less common flattened fauna, but see the following section on dangerous road animals before beginning that portion of your study. Birds (especially woodpeckers) and some mam-mals are described as "edge animals," living most commonly on the margin of forests. The occasional presence of some of the rarer road species, such as the flying (actually non-flying) squirrel (*Glaucomys* species) and the bushy-tailed wood rat (*Neotoma cinerea*) of the far Northwest, makes woodland and field-bordered roads with only moderate traffic loads a good choice for the novice, as well as for the expert.

Any road that you follow repeatedly while commuting to work or traveling to the local shopping area provides the opportunity to observe seasonal changes in species and abun-dance. Many of this guide's descriptions include information on seasonal presence. It's a good idea to keep written records of sightings and identifications along oft-traveled routes (see the final pages of the guide for record sheet format). As your death list grows, it is important to report rare specimens or dramatic changes in numbers to the International Simmons Society headquarters. Widespread sharing of information through the society will stimulate further interest in the road fauna and will increase general understanding and apprecia-tion for this up to now poorly known class of creatures.

While parking lots are not the best parts of the road habitat (they might be described as the deserts of the road), the occasional presence of a specimen of commonly flattened urban animals (such as the Norway rat or the house mouse) will provide a unique opportunity for the relatively safe, close-up examination of flattened fauna. Although close viewing or even collecting may be safer in parking lots than anywhere else (see following section on the collection of specimens), it is usually best to leave examples in place where they can be observed easily by other interested persons. Federal laws and many state laws prohibit the collection of any non-game animal without special permission. We can all help by refraining from collecting or disturbing the flattened fauna so that the animals can continue to educate the general public about the road's natural wonders. Let us not repeat the over-collecting errors of nineteenth-century naturalists and dilettantes; leave parking lot specimens in place. If you find something of exceptional interest, you might even encourage your local school's biology teachers to take the class on a field (or rather, road) trip. The urban environment is often all too poor in providing easily accessible examples of dead, two-dimensional things.

Collection of Road Specimens

Once you have become hooked on flat animals, the urge to collect representative specimens emerges quite naturally. You might even wish to prepare the particularly prime examples as wall mounts or paperweights. Resist that temptation! I have repeatedly discouraged the accumulation of flattened specimens by private collectors, although limited collecting for colleges and university museums might be acceptable. (Please check with the museum before delivering specimens and be certain that you have a Department of Highways collection license.[7])

There are at least five good reasons to limit collecting. First, the collection process is so dangerous in most situations that it is better left to the few expert flattened fauna collectors. Miscalculation of the speed of approaching vehicles is what created the road fauna in the first place, and there is little reason to risk adding yourself to the specimens already there. Second, fleas, mites, lice, and rabies, all of which can be acquired from too-fresh specimens, should discourage even

---

[7] Just kidding—there is no such thing as a Department of Highways Collection License; at least not yet.

the bravest student. Third, specimens in your private collection can no longer be enjoyed by the potentially thousands of road fauna students who are certainly behind you, guides in hand, and eyes on the road. Fourth, the necessary collection equipment is cumbersome, specialized, and seldom available to any but the serious professional. A heavy-duty scraper is essential and may have to be specially built, although a sturdy sidewalk ice-scraper will work for many smaller mammals and nearly all birds. And finally, in most states the possession of any non-game animal or bird is illegal, regardless of its condition. If you must collect, behave within the law and approach the task with all the caution and care that any dangerous activity requires.

A photographic record of specimens is often superior to the specimen itself, at least for ease of storage (photos are one of the few things flatter than the flattened animal, and digital storage removes any potential space constraints). The challenge of taking a clear photograph at highway speeds should stimulate even the seasoned camera buff. Although motion pictures or digital video are inappropriate to the subject matter, a good digital still camera should produce satisfactory results even at 55 mph.

Only bird identification is likely to be dependent on color, and most of the non-avian road fauna is protectively colored. That is, it more or less resembles the highway, especially after a few days. Flattened-fauna researchers are not certain whether the typical coloration is a specific adaptation to the road habitat, or whether it is merely accidental. Most think nearly everything that happens on the road is accidental, or at least not planned or designed.

How to Use This Book

In the interest of safety, the solitary driver should not attempt initial use of this guide. Bring a friend to use the key and the page numbers for the probable specimen spotted. More advanced students can probably dispense with the key on page 26 for all but the most confusing examples. As experience accumulates, it may be necessary only to refer to those illustrations of less frequently seen animals. Experienced solo drivers may keep the opened guide on the passenger seat and glance at the illustrations, but any more extensive use of the guide should be for the copilot or the soloist during rest stops.

Beginners and even advanced students will find it generally impossible to engage in long-term observation of a specimen in order to compare it to the illustrations and descriptions. By contrast with creatures from more stable habitats, members of the road fauna are ephemeral in at least two ways. First, the presence of any specimen in the road habitat is short term. The time between the animal's entry into the flattened mode and its disappearance from the road is brief. Depending on traffic and climatic factors (season, rainfall, etc.) anywhere from one to four days normally pass while the animal gradually becomes indistinguishable from the road surface. On Nebraska highways during the early 1940s, mean observation time was established at four days. On a major interstate in the twenty-first century, potential observation time may be measured in hours. Some medium-sized animals have remarkable persistence (see muskrats, page 70). Second, since the observer is generally in motion, the time available for making a single observation passes all too quickly. Five seconds is the measured average at highway speeds. Even in the unusual circumstance where you can stop briefly to examine the specimen, such observations must be done at a distance. The road habitat is far too dangerous for any leisurely contemplation of fine features. Most times, a brief look and spotting a couple of clear field marks or even a single salient feature must suffice.

Identification will sometimes be difficult and occasionally impossible. Only rough estimates of measurements can be made. Many of the descriptions and illustrations that follow emphasize single, critical identifying features. This guide is therefore much less complex than many field guides;

behavior or vocalizations are not prominently displayed by most flattened fauna.

The key on page 26 separates the road animals into four categories (mostly on the basis of single characteristics). And within each category the animals are listed by size, from smallest to largest. Comparisons with lane markers and painted stripes provide the only consistent size indication available in the five seconds from seeing to passing. A standard lane marker or no-passing yellow line is four and a half inches wide. When lane markers are presented on the illustrations, they are drawn to the same scale as the specimen.

Suggestions to facilitate more accurate identifications, given a longer examination time, are included for categories that contain many different species. However, I cannot over-emphasize the danger of careless inattention to genuine road-habitat hazards. Better to conclude that a particular specimen is probably a vole than to be certain it is *Microtus pennsylvanicus* and join it on the road.

Animal Posture and Presentation on the Road

Only a few representative photocopies and illustrations are provided for the snake, amphibian, and bird sections. Most birds assume such a multitude of shapes on the road that no single photocopy or silhouette will help in identification. Color characteristics are the critical features for birds, but the colors may be almost anywhere. Fortunately, the relative proportion of various colors remains consistent for most birds, and those proportions lend themselves more to verbal description than to any illustration.

Mammals, particularly those with more or less compact shapes, will develop only a few distinct patterns on the road. For those with short legs and a broad body, the usual pattern has one leg on each corner, with the flattening proceeding dorsi-ventrally (top to bottom). Badgers and woodchucks provide the best example of this pattern. They are so rarely found in a lateral presentation (on their side), with all legs extending in one direction, that no illustration of that posture is included. Larger animals or those with longer legs may be found in several typical postures. Genuine dorsi-ventral flattening is uncommon for rabbits, for example. They may be found with legs extending from the center in almost any direction. The silhouettes shown here (two or more are offered where appropriate) for most animals take into account presentational possibilities. Some mammal silhouettes are idealized patterns meant to help in pointing out specific identifying features, while others are photocopies of actual specimens. The latter are distinguished by their usually rougher outlines and somewhat more irregular shape.

It is impossible to represent all the variation found in a species, even with a number of illustrations. The problem is compounded in the case of flattened fauna by the rapid changes in form immediately following the animal's appearance on the road. The illustrations are not meant to encompass all possible variations, but to present, whenever possible, the form toward which that particular animal tends on the road. Even though the truly flattened specimen is as rare on the road as are ideal forms in the real world, it may be a useful philosophical concept. Animals of the road fauna clearly tend toward two dimensions, and the inherent beauty of a near-perfectly flattened creature must be seen to be appreciated. Serious photographers and even painters have just begun to recognize the artistic possibilities embodied in the animals of the road. The sense of serenity, even peacefulness, conveyed by a completely flattened animal provides an often startling, possibly meaningful, contrast to the barely controlled highway violence that produced it.

The flattest and somehow most persistent flat fauna of all are the few representations where the animal itself is long gone, but it somehow lingers in recognizable form. I know of only two examples. The first is the unmistakable shadow of a squirrel that had been flattened on a highway just before the machinery painting a new center stripe passed by. The squirrel, originally painted over, eventually disappeared, but the area where it had been retained the shadow of a squirrel until the next repainting of the center stripe. The only other known example was the image of a fast-flying pigeon on a seldom washed second story window of a chapel-auditorium at Luther College in Decorah, Iowa. The slightly oily feathers of the pigeon had been impressed onto the glass, and while feathers and bird were both gone, the tiny dust particles that had adhered to the oil imprint persisted for years; flat enough to be only vaguely visible with the right slant of light, but clearly a pigeon, with its wings spread and its head cocked quizzically to one side.

The Most Dangerous Animals on the Road

Your safaris into the road habitat will not be without danger, even if you stay in your car and proceed at speed limits. Any animal larger than a burly, adult raccoon is potentially life-threatening or at least vehicle damaging. Information about road fauna–caused accidents and fatalities is mostly available from North America, where our long-time romance with the automobile encourages us to keep track of such happenings.

Most of North America's large, wild mammals have been dramatically reduced in numbers, but there are exceptions. On a strictly numerical basis the North American white-tailed deer is much more dangerous than in any previous era and clearly the most dangerous animal on the highway. It is not as large as an elk nor as slow as a cow, but clearly "tis enough". The state of Michigan counts more than 50,000 deer-vehicle interactions per year; not unusual considering that in some locations deer populations may reach or exceed 70 animals per square mile. In the United States, the National Safety Council reported 29,000 motorists injured and 211 fatalities in on-road animal–vehicle crashes in 1995, nearly all of them involving white-tailed deer. Annually, an average of about 150 people die in the U.S. from deer-car crashes. By comparison, less than one person per year is injured or killed in attacks by bears, an animal we are likely to consider more dangerous.

For the numbers of animals actually present in the off-road habitat, moose are even more dangerous. While moose populations are always low, when they wander onto the road, they are truly frightening. An adult moose may weight 1500 pounds, and its legs are long enough to keep most of it above the usual motorist line-of-sight, particularly at night. The state of Maine has about 700 moose-car crashes per year and one-fourth of them result in serious injury or death to drivers and passengers. Of course, it is not good for the moose either.

The future in North America may hold some potential problems that have been absent as long as we have had highways. A consortium of environmental groups and some individuals (Nature Conservancy, World Wildlife Fund, Ted Turner, and the American Prairie Foundation) are engaged in a long-term plan to restore the animals and plants of the Great Plains from the Canadian border south to Nebraska. The expectation is that the American bison, elk, and other large mammals could be assisted to repopulate areas from which development and most human inhabitants would be excluded. Nearly 2 million acres are potentially involved. Highways will most certainly cross the area and a migrating herd of a few hundred bison would probably force an automobile off the road. Kind of like the problems faced in some of the African game parks, where an outraged rhinoceros can make a vehicle seem frail indeed.

Don't expect flattened bison any time soon, but it is well to plan for a probable future. North American roadways may become even more dangerous than they are now.

A Quick Key to the Major Groups of Flattened Fauna

What follows is called a dichotomous key, a standard device used in most guides and manuals to separate categories of plant or animal organisms. Each numbered "couplet" is meant to provide two statements that include all possible conditions and are mutually exclusive: feathers present versus feathers absent, for example. The numbers at the end of the statement tell you where to go next—either to a specific description on a numbered page or to the couplet with the next highest number.

1 Feathers present, often brightly colored, often flapping in the breeze from passing vehicles. **BIRDS, page 39**
   (If it has wings and no apparent feathers, see bats, page 58)

1 Feathers absent, seldom any bright colors and almost nothing flapping in the breeze. **2**

    2 More than 12 times longer than broad; no legs or other appendages. **SNAKES, page 27**

    2 Less than eight times longer than broad; leg, foot, or tail sometimes visible. **3**

        3 More or less fur-covered; fur sometimes visible only around the edges. **MAMMALS, page 57**

        3 No fur present (if animal is larger than twelve inches in any dimension and no fur is apparent, it may be a very old mammal or an armadillo).
        LEGGED REPTILES AND AMPHIBIANS, page 32

Size Determination

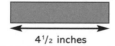

4½ inches
Scaled down lane marker

A standard lane marker or no-passing line is 4½ inches wide. Some of the illustrations and photocopies indicate the actual size of the specimen by showing an outline of a lane marker drawn to the same scale as the specimen.

chapter 3

Road Snakes

Snakes become part of the flattened fauna more commonly than their off-road numbers might indicate. Some herpetologists have suggested that nearly all snakes in heavily traveled parts of the country have found their way onto the road permanently, with a resultant reduction in their numbers off the road. Being cold-blooded, snakes will seek out warm places as the daily temperature cools, especially in the spring and fall. Before highways were built, they sought out large, flat, sun-warmed rocks, and stayed warm throughout the night. When asphalt and concrete highways were built, snakes must have felt grateful to the creators of such magnificent flat rocks—at least until the first car passed. In the golden age of herpetology, now long past, collectors could go out on new roads almost any spring or fall night and expect to find a satisfactory cross-section of live basking snakes. With increasing traffic, the only cross-sections to be found on the road are individual snakes that dozed off, evenings, on the warm asphalt. A reduction in snake numbers has paralleled the increase in highway construction—the snakes that remain have not yet come to terms with the automobile. Only the burrowing snakes are increasing in numbers.

Snakes present the most serious identification problem to be found on the road. Flattened snakes seldom show their colors to anyone who can't conduct a minute examination. Head shape and the presence or absence of specially shaped or divided individual scales do not survive the transition to flat. General body shape is similar for all snakes from the largest bull snake (*Pituophis melanoleucus*), eight feet long maximum, to the smallest ring-necked snake (*Diadophis punctatus*), less than one foot long. All snakes have a thick end and a thin end, with a more or less gradual taper in between. The challenge is to distinguish snakes as a group from any of the numerous long, narrow, non-animal objects that litter the highway (see "Mimicry"). Tree branches, bits of wire cable or rope, and long, thin fragments of tire tread may occasionally mimic snakes on the road. Precise observations of shape will nearly always separate snakes from other artifacts. Snakes, even when thoroughly flattened, are smooth for nearly their entire length, and on the ends as well. Artifacts, however, will show frayed edges or ends in almost every case. Most artifacts

One-half size. Photocopy by Canon NP-350F.

This photocopy represents most of the critical features of road snakes. The gradual taper toward the tail is characteristic, as is the slight enlargement of the head end. The curve of the body is the result of reflex movement and is more common than a nearly straight presentation. Given time and traffic, any snake can look like this, and almost no road mimic will show this whole combination of attributes.

will be of nearly uniform diameter for their whole length, while snakes are variously but consistently tapered.

Because so few species' characteristics survive flattening and baking, road snakes must be identified in general categories. The following pages distinguish small snakes from large snakes, and provide a list of the most likely victims nationwide in each category. Snakes that do retain some color or scale characteristics may be identified by close examination and reference to any of the standard live animal guides (see section on collecting specimens for instructions and cautions). Unlike with live snakes, you need not approach road snakes warily. No flattened snake is likely to attack, and very few of them are poisonous. However, do not stick your finger in the mouth of even the flattest snake.

SMALL SNAKES

Snakes whose length is less than five times the width of the road's yellow line are considered small snakes.

Garter Snakes (*Thamnophis* species)
12–18 inches

This may be the only snake you can identify on the road at highway speeds. All garter snakes have one or more clear, light-colored longitudinal stripes running the length of their bodies (they may appear as spirals in the older road forms). The stripes are usually visible for several days. Some species of garter snakes occur everywhere in the U.S. They are likely to be the second most common road snake (see "Large Snakes").

Green Snakes (*Opheodrys* species)
12–14 inches

Green snakes are sufficiently striking in color to be recognizable for nearly a day. Most are a uniform jade green color above, and white to yellow below. They are found everywhere except the mountain states and Pacific coast.

Ring-necked Snakes (*Diadophis punctatus*)
12–18 inches

These are small, almost totally nocturnal snakes. They are slate gray to black in color, with a yellowish to orange ring around the slender neck, and an orange to red underside at the tail end. The ring is not generally visible at any speed above 25 mph, but the undertail color can be seen at higher speeds. Both eastern and western forms occur, differing only slightly in the color and width of the neck ring and underside color patch.

LARGE SNAKES

Any snake extended a quarter or more of the width of a standard traffic lane is considered a large snake.

Bull Snakes (*Pituophis melanoleucus*)
5–8 feet

The bull snake can be found all over the U.S. and all over many highways. It is easily the most abundant snake on the road. H. Elliot McClure identified 398 bull snakes out of a total highway mortality list of 6,723 birds, mammals, and reptiles. Only toads were more common on McClure's list. The body is uniformly tapered and on the slim side for a temperate zone snake.

Garter Snakes (*Thamnophis* species)
3–4 feet

Most of the garter snakes on the road are young and inexperienced, but now and then a larger, older snake is caught napping.

Hognosed Snakes (*Heterodon* species)

The hognosed snakes are not common on the road, but may be recognized when seen. Along with rattlesnakes (see below), they are the most abundant thick-bodied snakes likely to be found from the Atlantic seaboard to the Rocky Mountains. Two characteristics deserve special mention. The hognose is the only snake that eats toads, and during a time of large-scale toad movement, it may be found with the toads on the roads. This snake will also "play possum" (see "opossum") and, if harassed by a near miss, will curl up and give a most convincing demonstration of lifelessness—a demonstration that almost inevitably turns into the real thing.

Rattlesnakes (*Crotalus* species)
3–8 feet

Rattlesnakes are unusual road residents except for in the southern Appalachians and the Southeast generally, where they are still abundant enough to equal the number of most other road-snake species. They are thick-bodied like the hognose and, when silent (as most are), are indistinguishable from them on the road.

Water Snakes (*Nerodia* species)
3–5 feet

Water snakes are aggressive and will not usually back down from a confrontation with anything. Their vigorous striking will often keep smaller predators at bay, but automobiles are notoriously unresponsive to their threats. Water snakes are dark, not dramatically marked, and about average in overall shape. Only the nearness of a pond or river will help suggest that the dark, tapered shape on the road might once have been an aggressive water snake.

chapter 4

Legged Reptiles and Amphibians

This is a composite category mostly because of processes that occur on the road. The pebbled surface of a flat toad cannot be distinguished from the scaled surface of a flat lizard or turtle at even the slowest observation speeds, and the thin-skinned frogs disappear from the road so quickly that they are not even included in the guide. If the road animal has (or appears to have had) four legs and lacks any evidence of fur, it probably belongs in this section. (Very old road mammals are often nearly bald except for a fringe of fur around the edges.) Reptiles and amphibians tend to appear hard-edged on the road. The only seriously problematic creature for most travelers is the southwestern armadillo. This is larger than all but the largest turtles you are likely to see on the road, and has a more elongated shape than any turtle (turtles do not generally elongate on the road). The armadillo's longer snout alone is often sufficient to distinguish it from any turtle.

Toads are the most common road animal in the "Legged Reptiles and Amphibians" category, although in special cir-cumstances turtles of particular species may be seasonally abundant. In McClure's study of Nebraska roads, toads were seen nine times as often as frogs or salamanders and approx-imately eight times as often as the most common turtle. Only rarely will lizards comprise anything but a minor com-ponent of the flattened fauna. An outbreak of road lizards

would be worth an immediate report to International Simmons Society headquarters.

The return of the American alligator (*Alligator mississippiensis*) to the highways of Florida must count as one of the
greatest comebacks in the history of road fauna. Twenty years
ago this creature was too rare to be worth mentioning. Its
flattened return to its former habitat must be viewed with
satisfaction.

ROAD TOADS
(Mostly genus *Bufo*)

HABITS AND ABUNDANCE In northern climates, spring
is the toad's breeding season, and large numbers of hormone-
high toads will be found on almost any road following early
spring rains. Any toad wishing to be represented in the next
generation must find a pool of shallow standing water and a
consenting toad of the opposite sex. Apparently not all toads
successfully make such a migration, considering the atten-
dant highway hazards. The same large, easily identifiable toad
has lived under our front porch for at least ten years; and
unless it sneaks away to a pond under cover of darkness and
returns quickly, it seems not to have felt the hormonal surge
that would send it journeying across any adjacent streets. It
remains safe but, I suspect, unfulfilled; it certainly won't leave
any offspring with the same stay-at-home tendencies. Southern toads breed at almost any time through the summer, and
toad traffic may be heavy following almost any downpour.
Among road fauna, toads are the only gregarious animals,
and will often be found in large numbers within a few feet of
one another.

Most natural predators avoid toads, as the toad's skin
contains glands that secrete distasteful milky substances. Feel-
ing safe from harm in most circumstances, a toad's natural
response to impending danger is likely to be hunkering down
rather than leaping away. This behavioral response produces
a more uniform road pattern for toads than for any other

creature in this guide. Flat toads are so nearly square as to be almost geometrical in their road presentation. Hognosed snakes seem to prefer toads, secretions and all, as food, and may be found in association with them on the road during toad migrations.

FIELD MARKS AND RANGE This common immobile amphibian is found in all parts of the country and in habitats ranging from plains to mountains to deserts. It is likely to be the first amphibian specimen the beginner will encounter. Visually similar but differently named species are found in

American toad (*Bufo americanus*)

The toad's tendency to flatten itself against the ground when threatened or afraid produces a uniform road pattern. The illustration is drawn from an actual specimen (male). Females are somewhat larger.

various geographic regions. Species are normally distinguished on the basis of color and minute anatomical features, none of which survives flattening. However, the rough, almost beaded-looking surface characteristic of nearly all species is persistent and diagnostic, even after days on the road. Road toads are generally dark and uniform in color, about three inches by three inches, with one limb usually visible at each corner. Often a forelimb is extended as though the toad were waving goodbye.

ROAD TURTLES

Turtles are historically significant. They entered the road fauna earlier than any other group. Any turtle that tries to get across a road, even with very slow-moving and sporadic traffic, is likely to become a permanent part of the scene. If a highway bisects the route turtles traditionally take to lay their eggs on some sandy spot, the road may resemble the site of a recent accident involving the Acme Casserole Company truck. Only a few kinds of turtles are likely to be identified as members of a particular species. A list of identifiable road turtles follows.

Painted Turtles (*Chrysemys picta*)
8–10 inches maximum diameter

Much of the color on the painted turtle's carapace, or shell (which gives this turtle its common name), does not survive the flattening process. Most specimens, however, will retain a bright red edge all around the shell. The shell itself is most often reduced to crumbled fragments, which look like a pile of dark crockery dropped from a considerable height. The painted turtle is found everywhere but in the Deep South.

Painted turtle (*Chrysemys picta*)

Turtles are, individually and as a group, so flat to start with that little dramatic shape change can be expected even after they have spent considerable time on the road. Slight variation in length of tail and extension of the head and neck will serve as aids in specific identification. Turtles begin and remain close to the road. The specimen shown is a male (identified by the large front claws). While this particular specimen is shown actual size, turtles of the same species can vary in size from about three inches to ten inches in length. Photocopy by Canon NP-350F.

Desert Tortoises or Gopher Tortoises (*Gopherus agassizi*)
12–14 inches maximum diameter

As the common name suggests, this turtle is restricted to the sandy areas of the Southwest. Most of these tortoises maintain separate feeding and hibernation areas and must travel from one to the other. New highways may cross the tortoises' usual paths and provide the best places to look for this once-common but now protected species.

Snapping Turtles (*Chelydra serpentina*)
18 inches maximum diameter

Snappers are almost totally aquatic, and they will be found on the road only during the spring egg-laying season. Compared to other turtles, their shells seem much too small for them, nor can their large head and long tail be retracted. The head and tail of a snapper will always be apparent on the road. Snapping turtles may be found during spring and fall anywhere in the eastern two-thirds of the country.

Soft-shell Turtles (*Trionyx* species)
14–24 inches maximum diameter

This is the only turtle that bends rather than breaks under the battering of the passing parade. If you find a uniformly oval spot, dark in color and appropriate in size, with just the hint of a long pointed nose at one end, it is likely to be a soft shell, especially on roads near rivers. It is found everywhere but the Rocky Mountains and the desert Southwest.

ALLIGATORS

American Alligators (*Alligator mississippiensis*)
1–4 feet long

This animal was once threatened with extinction, but it has made a dramatic comeback in recent decades. Now it is common enough to merit mention, even though its range is limited to Florida and the Gulf Coast.

HABITS AND ABUNDANCE The American alligator is nine inches long at hatching and leaves the nest while still young and near that size. The death rate for young animals is very high, as the highway attests. These alligators are never far from water, but where modern highways cut through swamps or near waterways, they cross roads as readily as they do any other bit of land. When small, they are potential food for many predators and so remain wary; but once they grow to about three feet (at about two years old), they begin to lose their fear and develop the aggressive behavior pattern that places so many animals on the road. By most standards, alligators are not smart, nor is any creature that approaches the road totally without fear.

FIELD MARKS AND RANGE The young alligator has vertical yellow stripes that are visible on the road for many days. Older animals lose the stripes and are uniformly dark, often resembling a large shoe or purse that someone has abandoned on the road, but with legs and a rough-edged tail. The alligator is found only in Florida and the Gulf states, with the exception of the occasional escaped or released pet in northern cities. An alligator seen on the streets of Boston or New York should immediately be reported to the International Simmons Society.

American alligator (*Alligator mississippiensis*)

No size indication is given with this silhouette, since the road alligator may be anywhere from a foot to four feet long and show exactly the same shape. Although the curve of the tail is not characteristic, it is often found in heavy traffic where a second car closely follows the first. The tail ridges shown here are characteristic and should be visible at highway speed.

chapter 5

Road Birds

The irregularly shaped splashes of color provided by birds set them apart as the most varied group of road fauna. Numerous studies have revealed that more species of birds end up on the road than any other single category of flattened fauna. Their numbers are not likely to be large in any one locality. However, two or three rare, documented, seasonally gregarious species—pine siskins (*Spinus pinus*) and both red- and white-winged crossbills (*Loxia curvirostra* and *Loxia leucoptera*)—have been reliably reported in large dead flocks on British Columbia roads in winter. More commonly, you will see single birds of various species. It is not unusual to encounter a dozen different species in a short late-summer outing on a good road. (See Introduction.)

Birds are the only part of the road fauna that show much of their original color in all conditions and ages on the road. They are distinguishable at a greater distance than most mammals and can be identified with no slowdown or delay. Subtleties of pattern will be lost as the flattening process proceeds (eye rings are seldom visible, for example), but major color patterns are retained for a long time with almost no loss of brilliance. A flat oriole provides a color contrast that is most welcome and distinctive on the generally drab highway surface. A bird cannot hide on the highway as it can in a forest or field. Our avian heritage is most observable in the flattened bird fauna, and birdwatching on the road is a fine way to begin understanding our feathered friends.

The birds listed in this section are in two major categories—urban birds and rural birds—paralleling the driving habits of most observers. You are most likely to encounter urban birds near cities or towns. Any overbuilt, human-inhabited area qualifies as urban; birds do not understand city speed limit signs. Within each major category the birds are listed by size, from smallest to largest.

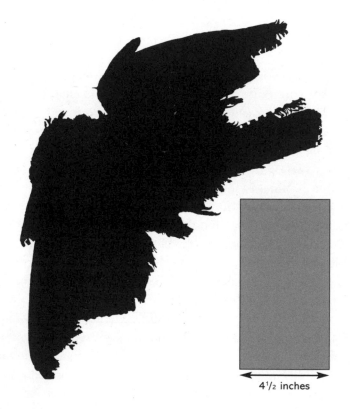

4¹/₂ inches

Belted kingfisher (*Megaceryle alcyon*)

Rarely, a bird will be captured on the road resembling its appearance in flight, apparently arrested in a split second of time. The arrested bird shown here is a belted kingfisher (*Megaceryle alcyon*), not otherwise described in the guide because of its rarity on the road. It is presented at the beginning of the bird section as an example of the sort of ideal specimen of any bird that readers might search for. Photocopy by Canon NP-350F.

URBAN BIRDS

House Sparrows (*Passer domesticus*)
5-inch body, 7-inch wings

HISTORY, HABITS, AND ABUNDANCE This import from Europe, which probably originated in Africa, is included among the urban birds mostly because of its history. It has lived with and near human dwellings for so long that its geographic origin is uncertain. From the earliest times, migrations of people have been accompanied by sparrows—especially once goats, cows, sheep, and horses were domesticated and dung became abundant near human dwellings. In the early 1850s a few sparrows were brought to the U.S. and released in several locations. By the 1870s every eastern city had huge flocks. The sparrows commonly fed in the streets, where undigested seeds in horse dung provided abundantly for their increasing numbers. Documentation is uncertain, but I believe the sparrow was the first bird to find its way into the road fauna. In 1862 in Philadelphia, on Chestnut Street, a lone male is reported to have been mashed under the wide wheels of a passing delivery wagon. The event caused widespread amazement, and was reported briefly in the local press. There is now some question whether the bird died a natural death and was later flattened, or whether it was actually caught by the passing wagon. Only God knows for sure about sparrows.

As trucks have replaced wagons on the streets of major eastern cities and the supply of fresh horse dung has diminished, the house sparrow has taken to the countryside and is now less abundant in cities than it was in 1900. Even though fewer urban sparrows are present, their abundance in the road fauna has remained constant or even increased, due mostly to the dramatic increase in speed and numbers of vehicles.

FIELD MARKS AND RANGE Sparrows have always followed horses, and large flocks can now often be seen near human dwellings in rural or near rural settings. Roads near a riding or boarding stable are fine places to look for outstanding specimens of this road resident. The sparrow is easily the

41

most common small bird in the entire road fauna. In 1938, Iowan Thomas Scott estimated that thirteen sparrows were plastered to each mile of highway there each year. The house sparrow is found throughout the U.S. and much of Canada, where it breeds during the entire year, except in the northern-most parts of its range.

On the road, prominent and dingy white patches of feath-ers will show for the first day or two, depending on the season (they last longer in winter). After than, most sparrows are pretty much road-colored, with few distinguishing features other than size and the lack of prominent color patches. Very few other sparrow species or birds of similar size are found on the road. If what you see is mostly gray or tan with some faint stripes and a bit of off-color white, and about six inches in maximum diameter, it most likely is (or was) a house sparrow.

Chimney Swifts (*Chaetura pelagica*)
5-inch body, 10-inch wings

HABITS AND ABUNDANCE Since this bird never sits or walks on the ground, it is not commonly a part of the road fauna. It is often seen in the air over cities, but the occasional road specimen may provide almost the only opportunity to see the bird at rest—it nearly never stops flying unless inter-cepted. It even collects twigs for its nest while in flight. The swift usually feeds on insects in the air, and occasionally fol-lows a potential meal into the headlight beams of a moving car at dawn or dusk, when it feeds most actively. Morning then finds the swift's gracefully bowed wings permanently impressed into the roadway. The bird's extraordinary speed on the wing prevails against hawks or owls, but it is evolu-tionarily unprepared for anything that moves as fast or looms as large as an automobile.

FIELD MARKS AND RANGE This graceful bird is found only during the summer in the eastern half of the U.S., where it lives close to civilization. Vaux's swift is the slightly smaller West Coast equivalent, but it is not an urban bird and is found only in dense forests. It has never been reported on the road. Chimney swifts once roosted and nested in caves, but they have found the brick chimneys of the urban East a nearly ideal habitat. Examples on the road are charcoal gray to black with a short body and long wings usually held in a crescent shape. No legs or feet are ever visible in road specimens. The usual highway silhouette is similar to that of the swallow or purple martin, but the martin is larger, with a longer body, and the swallow has much less gracefully curved wings and a much longer forked tail. The chimney swift is easily one of the most beautiful road birds.

While a swift in the air is common as dirt, a swift in the dirt is a finding rare enough to stop for and get a closer look. Resist the temptation however—especially at dawn or dusk. While you may be able to see the bird, other drivers may not be able to see you.

Starlings (*Sturnus vulgaris vulgaris*)
8-inch body, 12-inch wings

HABITS AND ABUNDANCE This European immigrant has made a place for itself, both in cities and countryside, more rapidly than anyone would have thought possible. In 1880, about eighty birds were introduced into New York City; now you can find that many in your back yard. Reportedly they were brought in to satisfy the whims of a Shakespeare Society that wanted all the birds mentioned in Shakespeare's plays to live everywhere on earth where the plays might be read or performed. We should probably continue to honor Shakespeare, but not necessarily his fans. By now, the starling is at home in the most thoroughly urban settings, and it is noisy, dirty, and pugnacious enough to drive other birds out of the neighborhood. (Its Latin name, *Sturnus vulgaris vulgaris*, fits both its commonness and its habits.) Many people view a starling on the road as worth at least two in the trees. Sheer numbers help explain why they are so abundant in the road fauna, but their catholic eating habits also contribute. Like many insect-eating birds, they feed on the road when pickings are slim in other places. Starlings are especially likely to be found spread out on the street during the nesting season, when they collect large numbers of insects to feed their developing young.

FIELD MARKS AND RANGE Starlings live nearly everywhere in the U.S., and they are present year-round over all but the northernmost parts of that range. If bill color can be determined at usual urban speeds, it is the best single field mark during the summer months, when the starling is the only black bird with a yellow bill. In winter the bill is dark, and the bird is heavily speckled. The mottled plumage, smaller size, shorter tail and urban proclivities will distinguish it from grackles and cowbirds. Most grackles and cowbirds migrate, however, so they aren't around when the starling is black-billed. Young starlings are only slightly mottled and nearly brown with lighter underparts. They are much more likely than adults to be found on the road. In most urban situations, any uniformly dark to slightly speckled bird about eight inches long is likely to be a starling. The wings, which are uniform black in the summer and brownish in the winter, often flap for days in the airstream of passing cars and trucks.

Northern Orioles (*Icterus galbula*)
7–8 inches

Some east-to-west variation in the details of color and pattern characterize this bird, but these details rapidly disappear on the road. Collectively, the orioles make up the most colorful and recognizable feathered road-residents.

HABITS AND ABUNDANCE The oriole builds its woven, hanging nest in tall trees overhanging open spaces. In a forest, this is just picturesque; in older neighborhoods, however, it is an invitation to disaster. Most of the appropriate trees extend out over residential streets, which brings the oriole into unwelcome contact with traffic—not frequently enough to produce caution but often enough to produce fatalities. The young, when hatched, set up a most persistent and audible call for food, and both parents may hear that particular note more clearly than the throaty murmur of an approaching Firebird.

FIELD MARKS AND RANGE An unmistakable combination half orange and half black, with only a few white lines visible on the occasionally flapping wings, mark this urban resident on the street surface. The oriole is found all across the country and into southern Canada in the summer. Although the oriole is found in both rural and urban areas, it is common enough on town and city streets to deserve designation as an urban bird. Small towns are the preferred place to look for well-developed specimens, although older city neighborhoods with mature trees are a good second choice.

Robins (*Turdus migratorius*)
10-inch body, 12-inch wings

HABITS AND ABUNDANCE In the northern U.S., the robin is most likely to find its way into the flattened fauna beginning in March, when it spends most of its time on lawns searching for insects and earthworms. When it attempts to cross the street to the next lawn, it is likely to be concentrating on the worm not yet in hand (or beak) rather than on the flow of traffic. Unfortunately, robins almost never fly across the street in spring—they run. This pedestrian approach to local travel keeps the robin population in check. During the winter months, large flocks of robins are characteristic in the Southeast and along the Gulf Coast. They often feed along roadsides and are at risk, like any flocking bird. The bird at the end of the group follows along and is wiped out (or wiped onto) the road surface. In the early part of the century, robins were hunted for food in the South ("Collect twenty-four robins, prepare a pie crust....").

FIELD MARKS AND RANGE The robin is found all across the country, and seasonally over most of North America. Some ornithologists distinguish a western variety, which is slightly different in color and somewhat larger, but none of the differences are observable by the time the fifth vehicle passes over the body. Any road robin found from west of the Great Plains to the Pacific Coast could be classified as the western variety without careful examination. Most often flattened male and female robins are about half medium brown and half red-orange, while juveniles are half brown and half speckled. The characteristic white eye-ring is not likely to be visible unless you are stopped for a traffic light.

Domestic Pigeons (*Columba livia*)
12-inch body, 16-inch wings

HABITS AND ABUNDANCE These common birds are almost synonymous with cities, although they are also frequent residents of farm buildings in rural areas. We are all familiar with wheeling flocks and feeding hordes of pigeons, but those permanently on the street receive less attention. Road pigeons are most common near parks and open plazas, demonstrating again that familiarity with humans and their artifacts can be unhealthy for animals. Pigeons don't usually feed directly on roads and streets, favoring sidewalks with discarded (or provided) popcorn. These birds are nonetheless at serious risk because of their numbers, their nearness to traveled roadways, and their flocking behavior. Individual birds in flocks are less wary of oncoming vehicles. Now and then a pigeon will simply lose track of its surroundings and fly into the side of a truck, having followed the flock to the point of no return. Pigeons are one of the few members of the road fauna likely to be intercepted by bicycles. Like many city birds, pigeons have come to regard humans as no threat, and a human on a bicycle must seem much like a human on the sidewalk. Pigeons are trusting creatures, to their detriment.

FIELD MARKS AND RANGE Pigeons are found everywhere in the U.S. and well into southern Canada. They do not migrate, but overwinter even in the northernmost parts of the range. They are thus one of a small number of birds as likely to appear in winter road inhabitant counts as summer ones.

Pigeons have been domesticated and selectively bred for centuries, so the color variation is enormous. However, nearly all have some bluish iridescence around the head and a black terminal tail band, both of which survive the severe flattening on urban streets. A small number of pigeons are white and lack both marks, but any totally white bird of this size must necessarily be a pigeon or a very small wandering chicken. No other bird of this size (about a foot wide—or slightly more in the second week) is so common on city streets in all seasons.

BOTH URBAN AND RURAL BIRDS

Common Crows (*Corvus brachyrynchos*)
18–20 inches

Like much of rural America, the crow has moved to town. This is the largest all-black bird to be found on the road; and while the rural representatives of this species are numerous, they are sufficiently cautious to be nearly unknown as permanent road fixtures. The growing urban crow populations of the past decade have developed the incautious habits of many urban birds and are now found in some numbers on city streets near parks and in tree-lined neighborhoods.

HABITS AND ABUNDANCE The crow eats anything from other, smaller birds, to eggs, vegetable material of many kinds, and most importantly for us, carrion found on roads. Rural crows are notably cautious, and in open country they will feed on road carrion and leave it well before any approaching vehicle threatens danger. In fact, crows are often one of the major reasons that other flattened birds and mammals do not remain on the road for very long. In cities where crow populations have increased dramatically, they seem to lose their rural apprehension and walk about on the street with some arrogance. Arrogance on the road is fatal. Young birds are particularly susceptible since they are slower and less agile flyers than adults. The last bite of a departed sparrow is often the last bite of anything for a young crow, if the rush hour coincides with the dinner hour. I have seen an urban crow spend ten minutes searching for and finally locating a discarded piece of pizza under a pile of autumn leaves on the edge of a busy street. Such persistence is fulfilling but hazardous.

FIELD MARKS AND RANGE The crow is abundant year-round in nearly all of North America and has taken to urban living (and dying) with a vengeance. Anything feathered, all black, larger than a pigeon, and on a city street is certain to be a crow. Watch for them in late May and early June when the young are fledged but not informed.

Herring Gulls (*Larus argentatus*)
20-inch body, wings never outstretched on the road

HABITS AND ABUNDANCE This most widely distributed of the gulls is a scavenger that will eat very nearly anything easy to get. Herring gulls commonly frequent the parking lots of fast-food emporiums and shores with picnic tables. Because of proximity to people, gulls have little fear of people, cars, trucks, trailers, or other fast-moving products of civilization. Herring gulls are exceptional flyers; but immature gulls (the only ones found on the road) often are less adept than they think and may find themselves caught in the downdraft of a passing truck. They are semigregarious, and many birds may often be found within a few hundred yards of one another.

FIELD MARKS AND RANGE The herring gull is found across the northern U.S. in the summer, and farther south along the coasts (where it is called the winter gull) in the colder months. The adults have a white head and tail, and gray wings with black tips. That striking color pattern is almost never seen on the road. For the first three years, the young are more or less mottled. Only in their third year do they begin to bear something more like their adult color. In no other bird is the preponderance of young on the road so great or so obvious. Any large, mottled white and dark bird on the road is likely to be an immature, no longer careless, herring gull. The feet, if visible, are pink.

The herring gull is neither genuinely urban nor committedly rural, but more a resort or vacation bird. It lives in all the places we would like to but can't afford. Maybe a diet of rotten fish and the hazards of the road are worth it.

The ring-billed gull, *Larus delawarensis*, is more common inland, especially around the Great Lakes. Adults are similar to the herring gull, but smaller (16-inch body), and the immature birds have a narrow black tail band often visible as separate dark-tipped feathers.

RURAL BIRDS

Red-winged Blackbirds (*Agelaius phoeniceus*)
7–8 inches

If roads that border marshes are good places to look for much of the road fauna, they are the perfect places to look for the red-winged blackbird. From early spring until late summer, these birds are solitary; but during the rest of the year they form huge flocks.

HABITS AND ABUNDANCE The very common and active red-wing needs only a small patch of cattails, tall grasses, weeds, or shrubs to claim as its own, and it often selects a roadside. The male (the only red-wing gender recognizable on the road) vigorously defends its small territory, and the females (up to six) nesting there. It will verbally abuse and even physically attack birds, mammals, and even people it views as potential threats to the space. Often the red-wing's concentration on an invading bird blinds it to other, more significant threats. A red-wing attempting to drive off a threatening crow may itself be driven on to the road by a passing Skylark. Since red-wings never feed on the road, they are likely to be intercepted in the air and may be carried some distance—the only explanation for their presence on the road a half mile or more from the nearest marsh. During the nesting season these are stay-at-home birds, except for the occasional summer auto trip on the front of that Skylark.

At migration time they travel in huge flocks, but roost in marshes and are seldom near roads. No matter what their Latin name suggests, once flattened, they rise again from the road as only a few wing feathers catching the breeze from passing trucks.

FIELD MARKS AND RANGE The red-wing's bright red-orange patch, with its thin yellow margin, can be seen on almost any road in the U.S. and much of Canada. The rest of the bird is a uniform black in any presentation. A red-wing cannot be flattened without one of the shoulder patches showing, which allows for instant recognition at any legal speed. In western California the tricolored blackbird (*Agelaius tricolor*), common on some marsh-bordered roads, is distinguished from the red-wing only by the white edge on the red shoulder patch.

Red-headed Woodpeckers (*Melanerpes erythrocephalus*)
9-inch body, 12-inch wings

HABITS AND ABUNDANCE The redhead is the most domestic of woodpeckers because it typically frequents forests that border human habitation. This preference creates a serious problem for the redhead when the forest edges and human dwellings are close to roads. The price of familiarity with humans is this bird's presence in the road fauna. Without question, the redhead is the most abundant woodpecker on the road, rivaled only by the yellow-shafted flicker (*Colaptes auratus*), which can be distinguished from the redhead by its larger size and gold-colored underwings. (See page 52.) The feeding habits of the redhead set it apart from most other woodpeckers and help to explain its preeminent place in the road fauna. While it will chip a beetle out of tree bark like its fellow woodpeckers, it frequently hauls its catch to some flat surface to soften it up before feeding. The redhead will also commonly eat insects that live on the ground (it enjoys ants, especially) or pursue flying grasshoppers and eat them on the wing. Corn on the cob is a favorite vegetable in season, which it finds along the roads. All this and a slow acceleration place the redhead at greater risk on the road than any other woodpecker. In 1932, Dr. Dayton Stoner reported thirty-nine redheads on 211 miles of highway.

FIELD MARKS AND RANGE Commonly present anywhere east of the Rocky Mountains, especially near open woods and fields, it is the only bird of the road fauna with a completely red head. The rest of the body and wings ordinarily show about equal amounts of clear white and deep blue-black. No matter how flat the bird may have been pressed by the passing parade, if you see something on the road that has feathers and is about equal parts of red, white, and black, you are looking at a red-headed woodpecker. Its ease of identification and abundance make the redhead a likely candidate to begin your death list of specimens. (See form on the inside back cover.)

Meadowlarks
(*Sturnella magna* [eastern] and *Sturnella neglecta* [western])
9 inches

Although their song is one of the important features that distinguish the two species, all meadowlarks are indistinguishable on the road. The state bird of Kansas, the meadowlark is one of the most common of the road fauna encountered in the summer there, and one of the most easily recognizable. Its beauty on the road is surely one reason why it is the state bird of five other states as well.

HABITS AND ABUNDANCE This bird's original home was in the tall- and short-grass prairies of the Midwest. As most of its grassy habitat was converted to corn and soybeans, and as hayfields disappeared when tractors replaced horses, more and more meadowlarks nested and fed in roadside ditches (the only habitat that remains unmowed during the nesting season). Their proximity to the highway, rather than any specific habits, produces the numbers of flat meadowlarks we commonly see. Young birds in this hazardous roadside habitat are particularly susceptible, and are most abundant on the road during June and July and again late in summer, since most meadowlarks attempt two broods in one season. Most of the young birds live only long enough to fly to the road.

FIELD MARKS AND RANGE The meadowlark is found from the East Coast to the West Coast and from Canada to Mexico, with a higher concentration in the Midwest. It winters in the South, as do many Midwesterners. The best single visible characteristic is the bright yellow breast. A bright yellow patch banded by black is nearly always visible in the well-developed road bird. The rest of the meadowlark is mottled tan, brown, and white. A nine-inch patch of feathers, a third of it yellow, will mark a meadowlark even for the beginner. Only the yellow-headed blackbird (*Xanthocephalus xanthocephalus*) of the West and Midwest is likely to be confused with the meadowlark. It is the same size and usually shows about the same amount of yellow, but the rest of the yellow-headed blackbird is nearly uniform black.

Yellow-shafted Flickers (*Colaptes auratus*)
11-inch body, 14-inch wings

HABITS AND ABUNDANCE The flicker feeds on the ground more than any other North American woodpecker and rests on the road more than any but the redhead. Ants may constitute 75 percent of the flicker's diet in some seasons. This bird will also pursue flying insects, a behavior that brings it into the path of fast-moving vehicles. Flickers are not aggressive birds, and many have been driven from their former urban homes by the more vigorous starlings. Flickers are now most commonly seen on roads near wooded regions, especially areas with farms, orchards, and isolated woodlots. In parts of the plains where trees are scarce, they will chip out nests in telephone or power poles, or even large fence posts. All these potential homes are nearer to traffic than would be best, especially for the young just beginning to develop flying and food-hunting skills. Playing near the road is never a good idea, and the number of young flickers permanently plastered there testifies to the danger.

FIELD MARKS AND RANGE The common northern flicker lives in the eastern two-thirds of the U.S., and as far north as Central Alaska. From the Rocky Mountains to the Pacific Coast, the red-shafted flicker is more common. Both are basically brown birds when seen on the road. The eastern flicker has a black bib and the nape of its neck is red. The western flicker has a red "mustache" and black bib. The golden-to-salmon color under their wings and tail is the only characteristic likely to be of much use after the first few cars have passed. If the bird happens to be right side up, a white rump patch is visible; if upside down, the black bib is obvious; and if lying on its side, only the wing and tail color will be useful.

Road Runners (*Geococcyx californianus*)
22 inches long (half tail)

HABITS AND ABUNDANCE This is a less common inhabitant of the road than most other birds in the guide, but its close association with highways and traffic demand its inclusion. The road runner is capable of outdistancing a team of running horses, and early reports suggest that the birds seemed to enjoy these races. They would clearly rather run than fly, but even the earliest automobiles and trucks were faster than these birds expected. Its food consists mostly of lizards and small snakes, with insects and even an occasional small bird as an important supplement. The road runner occasionally feeds on carrion, which makes it especially likely to enter the road fauna during early summer and late fall, when lizards and snakes (before they become part of the flattened fauna themselves) seek the warmth of the road in the evening and early morning. When feeding its growing young in midsummer, this bird will recklessly follow lizards out onto the road surface, where occasionally both become road ornaments rather than road runners.

FIELD MARKS AND RANGE Although the road runner is often described as a striking bird, more often it is a struck bird. It bears strongly mottled plumage, which is remarkably good camouflage in regions of strong sunlight and sparse plant cover. The plumage is coarse, white above and dark below, although on the road the colors could be mixed. The road runner is not a compact bird, and on the road it often looks like something has surprised it—it tends to seem more scattered than most birds. The only bird in the Southwest likely to be confused with it is the magpie (*Picapicaalso hudsonicus*), which also has a long tail but is slightly smaller and shows dramatic white wing patches in all road conditions.

4¹/₂ inches

Road runner (*Geococcyx californianus*)

This illustration was drawn from a dead road runner and is included to show something of the serenity achieved by a few road animals. The frantic pace of constant food-seeking has slowed considerably here. Regardless of traffic speed, the bird is clearly at rest.

Barn Owls (*Tyto alba*)
14–18 inches

The barn owl and its near relatives live and die over nearly all the temperate and tropical world, but are so secretive that they are less well known than almost any other birds their size. A barn owl on the road may provide almost the only opportunity to get even a brief daylight glimpse of this unusual predator.

HABITS AND ABUNDANCE As with many other members of the flattened fauna, association with human civilization and its artifacts can be fatal to barn owls. They ordinarily roost and nest in abandoned buildings well away from forests, flying out to feed only after dark. They cruise low and silently over open spaces, looking for rodents (their principal food), crossing and even paralleling roads and road edges. Lights of any kind, particularly moving lights, will disorient this bird. Their evolution as night hunters has in no way prepared them for the abrupt transition from darkness to the dazzling headlights of an eighteen-wheeler lumbering down the road. (Confusion on the highway is fatal to many animals, and the barn owl is no exception.) The combination of strictly nocturnal habits and nearness to human dwellings makes the barn owl more susceptible than most to late-night traffic.

FIELD MARKS AND RANGE The barn owl is uncommon in the northern and mountain states, but is abundant over much of the country. It prefers warm climates; it is common in California, where it appears to have resettled, along with other Midwesterners. The barn owl's legs are long enough to be obvious on almost any road specimen. Those, along with the white- to light-colored facial mask, are the dominant features. Time of day may be critical in identification. If the specimen wasn't there the night before, or if it is about fourteen to eighteen inches across and mostly white or light in color, chances are you have spotted a barn owl. During daylight hours they are more properly called "road owls," since they seldom are seen anywhere else. No other owl is so common on the road.

Ring-necked Pheasants
(*Phasianus colchicus*)
24 inches plus

No other road bird displays the brilliant plumage and long tail of this immigrant. As with many immigrants, its origin is uncertain and its ancestry mixed. The bird presently found on our highways is a mixture of English, Chinese, and probably Middle Eastern forebears (or forepheasants) that have adapted well, spread widely, and reproduced extensively since arrival in the U.S. in the 1880s and 1890s.

HABITS AND ABUNDANCE The pheasant is active year-round, and it often finds the most suitable habitat at roadsides and in road ditches near cultivated fields. The ditch's unmown grass provides cover for the simple nest, and the gravel,[8] discarded grain, and insects of the road edge provide the necessities of daily life. When snow covers much of the feeding areas in fields, flocks of pheasants are almost confined to the road edge during daylight hours. They are fast but not agile flyers, and many road pheasants are first struck while trying to fly from one road edge to another. Why the pheasant crosses the road is a question with no easy answer, but the fact that it attempts to do so often is obvious.

FIELD MARKS AND RANGE The male's iridescent purple head, prominent white neck ring, bronze-to-greenish body, and extremely long tail are reliable marks in almost any road condition. The foot-long tail feathers banded in tan and brown are almost never bent or broken by even severe impact, and constitute the best single feature. The females are a uniform mottled brown, but share the long tail. The pheasant on the road is most common in the Great Plains and is found more often than any other bird in several states including South Dakota and Nebraska. They occur only sporadically in the South and far West.

---

[8] The pheasant, like other gallinaceous (chicken-like) birds, needs gravel for its gizzard, where the gravel helps grind up the seeds in the diet.

chapter 6

Road Mammals

This section lists mammals by size, from smallest to largest. The largest mammals treated in detail are raccoons, even though they are only marginally flattened in most cases. In animals larger than the marmot, the flattening process is complex; in some cases it produces a shape more like a spiral than the simpler forms illustrated there. For example, the longitudinal stripes of a skunk may in come cases appear as a series of diagonal white lines crossing the long axis of the body. Any large, partially flattened animal may produce a pattern too confusing for identification.

Since mammals of all sizes are clearly killed along the road, some mention of the larger species of mammals may be helpful, even though they never become part of the flattened fauna. Not only do the larger creatures rarely present the nearly two-dimensional character of the true road fauna (*Fauna itinerarius*), but also most often they are not found on the road proper but only on its margins. Some authorities suggest that the larger mammals should be considered "edge" species, characteristically occupying the habitat between the road proper and the surrounding countryside.

Among the larger forms—moose, elk, deer, antelope, caribou, bison, bear, and wolves—only the white-tailed dear of the eastern U.S. is likely to be encountered often enough to be worth specific mention. Each year, thousands of these animals join the ranks of the fauna that, if not flattened, are at least somewhat compressed. Most road fatalities are the result of the deer's normal behavior patterns, and its inability to adjust to a new habitat (the road) and a new predator (the automobile). Deer are crepuscular, which means they are most active around dusk or twilight, a time when drivers don't see as well and when lights are most likely to confuse the deer. Deer also frequent forest edges—safe places to be in a roadless wilderness—since they can see potential predators at some distance, and since food of edible height is plentiful. As eastern forests were cleared for agriculture, and as roads crisscrossed the deer's normal range, the amount of forest edge—much of it adjacent to high-speed traffic—has increased. A deer that can clear an eight-foot obstacle from a standing start could easily leap over a moving car; but few deer recognize vehicles as a specific danger until too late. Young deer are especially susceptible, and are disproportionately represented on highway edges.

Drivers interested specifically in the mammals of the road fauna are hereby warned that the larger forms are genuinely dangerous. Fixing a squirrel on the road for later study might be an excusable, if morally reprehensible, act; but any creature of beaver-size or larger represents a significant hazard to vehicle and driver. In an interesting reversal of the usual pattern by which creatures enter the flattened fauna, a deer, bear, or equivalent-sized animal has a fair shot at flattening at least some part of the vehicle involved in such an encounter—and in some cases, flattening the drivers as well. Next to drivers, deer and other large mammals are the most dangerous creatures likely to be encountered on the road.

Bats (order *Chiroptera*)

Various genera and dozens of species. Wings are mostly 9–12 inches across, but because of folding, most bats on the road are less than 9 inches maximum dimension.

HABITS AND ABUNDANCE No creature of the road fauna is as close to the road as the bat and yet few people who travel the U.S. highways will be aware of them. Nearly all bats weigh less than an ounce and, spread on the road, they are thin, hardly visible, and very seldom identifiable to the auto traveler. For the biker and hiker, however, bats can contribute significantly to the road scene. William F. Adams of Wilmington, North Carolina, studies the road fauna from a bicycle. He suggests that most road bats were hunting insects along the length of the road, much as they do when they fly down the course of small rivers and creeks to locate their food. Roads with forests on both sides are prime habitat for many species of highway bats. Bats locate their flying insect prey with a kind of radar and are capable of following the erratic path of a flying insect in complete darkness until they snatch it from the air and eat it on the wing. Such concentration on nontraffic matters while flying along a highway can be quickly fatal. The bat's evolutionary adaptations have no responses to creatures as large or as fast as a car, and even if they did, radar doesn't work as well for avoiding moving objects as it does for following them. Since bats often fly higher off the ground than the height of most automobiles, they are often the victims of taller trucks. A truck near a bat zeroing in on a moth will almost certainly overload the bat's radar system. A bat near the centerline of a forest-edged road, concentrating on a fluttering moth, may never be aware of the vehicle that turns it into what often looks like an irregularly shaped piece of black plastic on the road surface.

FIELD MARKS No creature on the road is so variably shaped as the bat. They are almost always folded over on themselves several times. Some appear nearly circular; others may look like a bit of dark cloth cut into a six-pointed star. The following silhouettes suggest something of an average initial shape, but after a day or less, they will assume the detailed contours of the road and will often be indistinguishable by either color or shape.

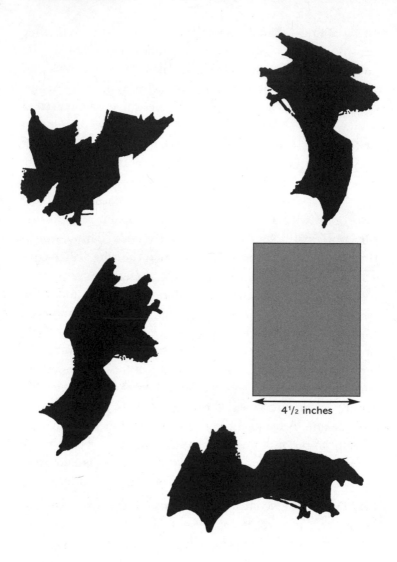

4¹/₂ inches

Bats (order *Chiroptera*)

Road bats can look like almost anything. If these black shapes seem like dirty pictures to you, don't spend too much time looking for *Chiroptera*. Road bats vary in size from less than six inches to more than twelve inches across. The scale marker shown would fit most of the common bats found north of Mexico.

Mice and Voles (family Cricetidae)
2–3 inches x 4–6 inches, with long, usually hairless tail

About twenty species in North America make up the family Cricetidae. *Cricetid* means hamsterlike. These are the smallest visible members of the road fauna, on the average even smaller than the width of the yellow line, although a few may be as long as six inches. (The eastern woodrat, *Neotoma floridana*, may be nearly nine inches long.) Most Cricetids will be easier to spot by bikers and hikers than by drivers.

HABITS AND ABUNDANCE Considered collectively, mice and voles eat nearly anything, breed prolifically, and are subject to population explosions when conditions are right. A single species may have a population in the hundreds per acre, and even though they live for only a few months before dying from predation or old age, they are nowhere near as abundant on the road as their field numbers might indicate. Most are stay-at-homes who don't travel any distance or in any numbers unless conditions have become intolerable, such as when seventy-five cousins and brothers-in-law move into the old nest. When out of their burrows, mice and voles demonstrate what is called wall-seeking behavior: an overpowering urge to be near some vertical surface. This keeps most of them off the road. The meadow vole (*Microtus pennsylvanicus*) is capable of producing populations that may number in the thousands per acre for a short time, until snakes, owls, hawks, and even Firebirds, Cougars, Jaguars, and Foxes flatten out the population curve.

FIELD MARKS AND RANGE Many of the mice and voles are so uniform in color that even close examination reveals only a three-by-five-inch spot roughly the color of a weathered asphalt surface. The large bulging eyes common to most of the small mammals will be visible only to very slow-moving traffic. The deer mouse (*Peromyscus* species) and some of the woodrats (*Neotoma* species) have contrasting white underparts that may show on the road. Numerous species of mice and voles are present in every corner (next to the wall) of North America, with the widest variety in the Southeast.

Do not even bother trying to identify any of the mice and voles on the road: identifying marks are gone quickly, and the dangers of slowing down are not worth the minimal rewards of adding yet another Cricetid to your death list.

The shrews (family Soricidae) are about the size of mice and voles, but as carnivores they are much less numerous in the fields and on the roads. Only the elongated nose will distinguish the road shrew from the road vole. (See illustration.)

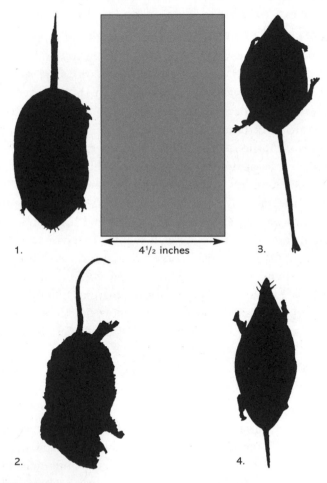

1. Vole, dorsi-ventral presentation.
2. House mouse, lateral presentation (photocopy by Canon NP-350F).
3. Deer mouse, dorsi-ventral presentation.
4. Short-tailed shrew.

Eastern Chipmunks (*Tamias striatus*)
5 x 2 inches, with a 3-inch short-furred tail

HABITS AND ABUNDANCE Over all of eastern North America, the chipmunk is found in brushy parts of deciduous forests, often in parks and campgrounds. Chipmunks are likely to forage along roadsides and often have little fear of people or cars. They normally eat nuts, berries, and acorns, but will not scorn a bit of road carrion, even that of a near relative. In autumn they accumulate food for the winter and are busy enough to be distracted from even minimal concern with traffic. In early spring, their mating chases will also distract these animals from watching out for automobiles. Chipmunks are occasionally found together in pairs on the road during mating season. The young leave the parental burrow at five or

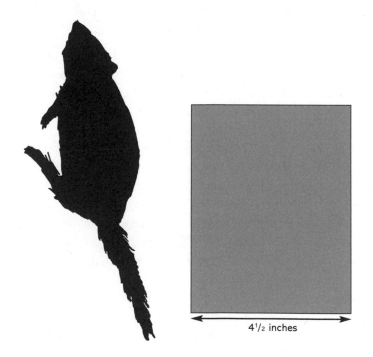

4¹/₂ inches

Eastern chipmunk (*Tamias striatus*)

The chipmunk has so little substance inside its fur that its shape on the road closely resembles its shape in the woods. Its size and the presence of light-colored longitudinal stripes sets this animal apart from any mimics.

63

six weeks and often travel long distances. The combination of naivete and vacation traffic makes this attractive little mammal abundant on the road. The chipmunk hibernates in the northern parts of its range, but it may be found on roads alongside parks and woods in all seasons further south.

FIELD MARKS AND RANGE The eastern chipmunk is by far the most common small mammal on urban park roads, but several western species (very similar when flat) occur in mountainous areas. All species show similar longitudinal stripes on a background of tan to brown. The road chipmunk usually reveals a pointed nose and a slightly bushy tail. Feet and ears are not likely to be visible.

Thirteen-lined Ground Squirrels (*Spermophilus tridecemlineatus*)
6 x 2 inches, with a 3-inch short-furred tail

HABITS AND ABUNDANCE This, the most common road squirrel of the central U.S., is commonly called a "gopher." These squirrels of the plains states are curious animals who will often stand up on their hind legs and stare at an approaching car before leaving the food that lured them onto the road (and often keeps them there for several days). Their varied diet consists of seeds blown off grain trucks, insects bounced off cars, and occasionally carrion already flattened by previous passersby. Their abandoned burrows can often be found at the edge of vegetation just off the road shoulder. When sufficiently flattened, they can leave the asphalt by "road drift" to the shoulder, where they will remain for several weeks in dry weather. The young, particularly abundant during late summer, are more commonly found on the road than adults. The gopher is a true hibernator and spends all the cold months in a state of suspended animation far from the road.

FIELD MARKS AND RANGE Their body shape is nearly rectangular, with parallel sides for nearly the entire six-inch length. The numerous light-colored longitudinal lines and rows of spots on a tan-to-medium-brown body may be oriented lengthwise or diagonally, depending on the violence of the animal's demise. They are found from Ohio to Wyoming, and from southern Canada to Texas.

If the animal seen is about the same size as the thirteen-lined ground squirrel, but has the fewer stripes characteristic of the slightly smaller and less rectangular eastern chipmunk, it is probably a gold-mantled ground squirrel (*Spermophilus*

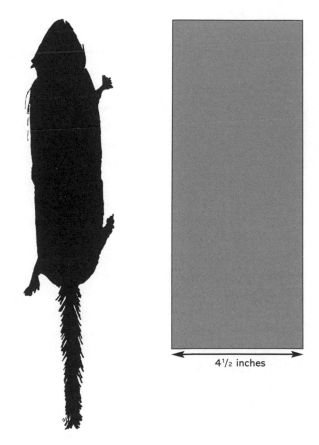

4¹/₂ inches

Thirteen-lined ground squirrel (*Spermophilus tridecemlineatus*), commonly known as a gopher

No road mammal has the longitudinal extension of the thirteen-lined ground squirrel. You don't need to count all thirteen lines; nothing else on the road has more than four lengthwise stripes, and only a snake is as long and narrow.

lateralis). This common resident of the mountain states hangs around campgrounds and picnic areas. It is often seen decorating western roadways near high human-use areas. Any close association with people is likely to introduce an animal into the road fauna. Where there are people, there are fast-moving wheels and flattened squirrels.

Norway Rats (*Rattus norvegicus*)
9 x 4 inches, with a 9-inch hairless tail

HABITS AND ABUNDANCE Wherever people live, the equally adaptable Norway rat follows and establishes itself. It learns quickly and is probably more vehicle-shy than any other mammal; it seems to have lived with us long enough to appreciate the hazards of automobiles and trucks. Five or six litters in a single year and year-round breeding in all climates are characteristic: A single pair of rats can produce 1,000 descendants in a single year. Norway rats don't generally live for more than a few months, but even so, numbers in any urban area can be in the thousands per block. We might therefore expect the highways passing through high urban concentrations to be nearly covered with flat rats, but such is not the case. This suggests that these rats have adapted to highways and people unlike any other animal in the guide. Rats are vastly underrepresented in any road fauna sample, even though they may be living under or even on the road. An individual or even a small family will occasionally take up residence in a larger car or truck and live on potato chip crumbs and discarded Big Macs, becoming the only member of the road fauna known to use vehicles for transportation. Young males wander for considerable distances and are the specimens most commonly seen on urban streets. These are one of the few flattened fauna members seen in parking lots.

FIELD MARKS AND RANGE Norway rats are a uniform gray and present an elongated oval shape after a short time on the road or in the parking lot. Their size and hairless tail will distinguish them. All the rats native to this continent

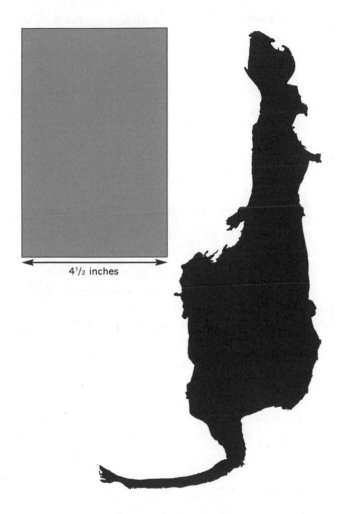

4¹/₂ inches

Norway rat (*Rattus norvegicus*)

This is a parking-lot rat, and an old one. Size, the visible dentition, and the hairless tail pinpoint the identification. Parking-lot animals can be examined at leisure, and features like dentition become significant on close scrutiny. Photocopy by Canon NP-350F.

are somewhat smaller, have furrier tails, and are not likely to be found in urban locations. The Norway rat is never far from where people live. The smaller, more slender, and darker black rat (*Rattus rattus*) is confined to harbors and near-harbor urban areas, particularly on the south Atlantic and California coasts.

Tree Squirrels (*Sciurus* species)
14 x 6 inches, with a bushy tail as long as the body

HABITS AND ABUNDANCE While wooded areas in the countryside are home to large numbers of squirrels, long-settled urban areas provide nearly all the road specimens. Urban squirrels are almost totally unwary of human activity and pay a high price for their casual approach, especially the young ones. With the abundant nuts and fruits available in most urban areas and parks, many squirrels are so well nourished that they produce two litters per year, making the young animals likely to be reduced to two dimensions abundant almost year-round. The young are most active in June and October, especially in the latter month, when in addition to learning to feed themselves they begin to store food for the winter. Adult males are most likely to become part of the road fauna in January and June when they regularly chase females for hours at a time. Often several males will chase a single female, and their minds are certainly not on traffic patterns. Natural selection may operate clearly here, as the slowest male is most at risk. As one naturalist puts it, "The trailing male is clearly on the paving." Population eruptions and mass movements involving hundreds of squirrels have been reported only rarely. Here, too, the squirrels appear to not be concentrating on safety, and may be found flattened by the dozens in a single mile. Squirrels are crepuscular (most active at dawn and dusk), which in many seasons put them on the road at the busiest times. They have a sufficiently keen sense of smell to find acorns under a foot of snow, but this sense is useless when it comes to moving objects.

FIELD MARKS AND RANGE Color and pattern vary both within and between species, and the color variation is most dramatic in urban populations, from the pure white squirrels of Olney, Illinois, to occasional black ones. Most are nearly uniform tan to red or brown, with somewhat lighter under-parts. A nearly uniform patch of appropriately sized fur with a long bushy tail will almost always mark a road squirrel, even if no other features are discernible. The tail remains free of the road and waves conspicuously in the slipstream from passing traffic. The squirrel is one of the few mammals that shows much movement on the road.

4½ inches

Tree squirrel (*Sciurus* species)

Squirrels present about equally in lateral or dorsi-ventral positions. The tail is never folded, and an average of three legs should be visible on any road specimen.

One or another of the species of *Sciurus*, or their near relatives *Tamiasciurus* (including the Douglas squirrel of the Pacific Northwest and the northern red squirrel of the northern U.S. and Canada), is found all across the U.S. wherever trees are available. The grey squirrels (*Sciurus carolinensis*) and fox squirrels (*Sciurus niger*), most common on the residential streets, are found mostly in the eastern half of the country. Members of transplanted populations of both species appear on roads near parks and parklike areas on the West Coast.

Muskrats (*Ondatra zibethicus*)
12 x 8 inches, with a 12-inch hairless tail

HABITS AND ABUNDANCE The muskrat never feeds on the road, but is present in large enough numbers in spring and fall to be near the top of anyone's road species list. It eats marsh plants (with the exception noted below), and as part of the road fauna, will most likely be found by marsh-bordered roads. However, during spring and fall it migrates long distances between marshes and may be found anywhere, including garage driveways in large cities. The period of dispersal is longer and more pronounced if muskrat populations are high, and under favorable conditions a pair of muskrats can become two dozen in a single season. With high population levels and competition for food, cannibalism is a real option for muskrats, and many of the younger muskrats would apparently rather be Chevettized than cannibalized. The young are often driven out of the marsh by older muskrats at about six weeks of age, when they must attempt to find new homes—often a spot on the highway or even a place in the suburbs. They are comfortable with humans and human activities and may be found in large numbers even in cities, if marshy land with standing water is available. Their usual response to perceived danger is to dive in and swim away under water. On land they are much more aggressive, but on the road this is a fatal character flaw.

FIELD MARKS AND RANGE The muskrat has a thick, strong, darkly furred pelt. The animal holds together well and assumes a nearly constant shape on the road. The short front legs are seldom obvious (now and then a back foot may be visible; see silhouette, below), the back feet are webbed, and no neck or ears are visible. The usual shape is a near-perfect oval, slightly pointed on the head end, with a long, flattened tail. The color is uniform over the oval and varies from reddish to dark brown.

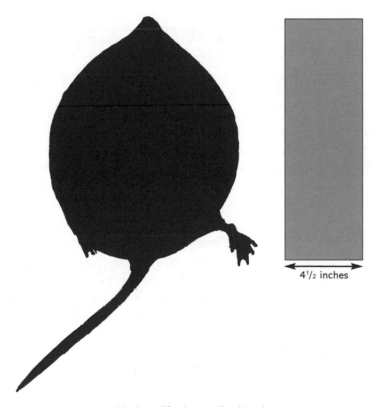

4 ¹/₂ inches

Muskrat (*Ondatra zibethicus*)

A prime muskrat pelt is one of the more durable and dependable items on the road. Most muskrats, regardless of their status at initial impact, develop rapidly into the nearly round silhouette shown here. Only an opossum, which is more elongated on the road, could be confused with a road muskrat. The muskrat's webbed feet determine the diagnosis and should be easily identifiable to a biker or hiker.

Muskrats occur in every state except Hawaii. Along the Gulf Coast and in coastal Washington and Oregon, what looks like an overly large muskrat on the road may be a nutria (*Myocastor coypus*), a sometimes abundant Argentinean import that has escaped captivity and established itself in marshy locations. It has a more obvious neck and a more nearly square road form.

Opossums (*Didelphis virginiana*)
20 x 12 inches, with a 12-inch hairless tail

HABITS AND ABUNDANCE Contrary to popular southern opinion, opossums are not born dead by the side of the road, but may give that impression in places where they are abundant. The opossum often forages on the road and may briefly benefit from the varied diet available there. It will literally eat anything, including its relatives who were feeding on the road a few days earlier. In their off-road habitat, opossums are too tough to kill easily (serious reports suggest that they are immune to rattlesnake venom), and many a dog has mauled or left for dead an opossum that went on its way once the dog departed. But on the road the opossum's toughness may work to its disadvantage. Becoming limp and lying there with an open mouth after a near miss by the first car may serve to put off a dog or coyote, but stands little chance against even compact cars. Such behavior is surely fatal on the road, where lying down quickly becomes a permanent condition. There is often not enough time to play dead before becoming dead. A nocturnal activity pattern and a fascination with approaching lights also serves to increase the road opossum population. Even without cars, usually opossums live for no more than two years, which is not enough time to learn much about traffic patterns. Nomadic males less than a year old are particularly common on the road. Overall, the opossum is the most abundant mammal of its size on the road, by virtue of its ability to adapt to nearly any surroundings and a tendency to stand and fight when confronted.

FIELD MARKS AND RANGE Since early times of European settlement in the U.S., the opossum has spread from its original southeastern home to the Canadian border, and now is found in all but the mountain states of the West. It was introduced in California in 1870, and thrives there in association with human activities of all kinds. Opossums do not

4¹/₂ inches

Opossum (*Didelphis virginiana*)

The light color and elongated shape distinguish the opossum from its near road relatives. The hairs spread out in all directions on the road.

hibernate and, in more northerly parts of their current range, winter opossums may display severely frostbitten ears and tails even before they settle onto the road. The opossum is as likely to be found in urban as rural environments. In urban areas it will raid garbage cans to get the varied diet it prefers. According to Tom Torgerson of Eureka, California, a serious, longtime student of the California road fauna, a road opossum looks like a cat that stuck its paw in a light socket. It is almost the size of a house cat and does present a scruffy appearance, due to its long, grizzled hair. The road shape is a nearly uniform oval even after a few passes from an eighteen-wheeler. It tapers at one end to a hairless foot-long tail, and at the other to a pointed, whiskery snout. Its color is a nearly uniform gray with some longer white-tipped hairs. Individual color varies from nearly white to the rare cinnamon opossum.

Woodchuck (also called groundhog) (*Marmota monax*)
18 x 12 inches, with a 9-inch bushy tail

The largest of the ground squirrels is one of the few animals whose habitat has been enhanced by human activities. Naturalists describe woodchucks as "edge" organisms. Clearing the forests in the eastern half of the U.S. for agriculture and civilized pursuits has created new edges and new habitat, much of it right on the edge of roads and highways. The woodchuck is much more common now over its geographic range than it was in colonial times. There are several western species of *Marmota*, but they are mostly restricted to high altitudes and are extremely rare on the road.

HABITS AND ABUNDANCE Considering the numbers and their usual proximity to roadways, woodchucks are underrepresented in the road fauna. They have excellent eyesight, forage only during daylight hours, sleep most of the time, hibernate for six months of the year, never travel far from their burrows, and have reasonably good speed afoot. However, their typical times of foraging coincide closely with daily rush hours, and the young tend to be uninformed about speed limits and road hazards. The elders usually drive the young out of the paternal burrow at the end of summer, by that time having had enough of five or six kids underfoot in cramped quarters. Most adult woodchucks are totally solitary in habits (except for a brief breeding season) and extremely aggressive

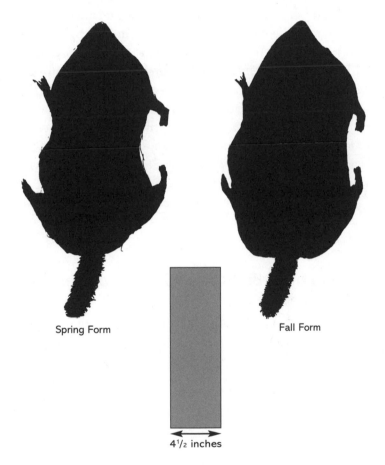

Spring Form   Fall Form

4¹/₂ inches

Woodchuck (*Marmota monax*)

Woodchucks on the road are nearly all dorsi-ventral in presentation. The chuck on the left demonstrates the spring appearance after a winter's hibernation, and looks much like the shadow you might expect to see on February 2nd. The one on the right shows what summer eating will do for your silhouette.

toward other woodchucks, although they will flee from auto-mobiles. Over the northern part of their range, they hibernate throughout the cold months and are never found on the road at that time. In early spring, however, they may venture onto smooth surfaces, looking for a clear shadow of themselves. The shadow and the silhouette are similar (see page 75).

FIELD MARKS AND RANGE The woodchuck is heavy bodied and short-legged, usually presenting an almost square appearance. The color is a nearly uniform brown to yellow brown, and somewhat grizzled—the coat has long guard hairs with light-colored ends. The feet are dark to almost black. Most roadchucks are larger than a squirrel and smaller than a badger or raccoon. Fall roadchucks are considerably wider than early summer specimens, since they store large amounts of fat for winter hibernation. Most of the chucks seen on the road in late summer are more square than rectangular, with their dark feet barely visible at the corners.

Woodchucks are common over the eastern half of the U.S. except for the southeast coastal plain; they are absent from Florida and Louisiana.

Cottontail Rabbits (*Sylvilagus* species)
16 x 16 inches

HABITS AND ABUNDANCE The habits of rabbits do not bring them often to the road, but sheer numbers assure that they will be abundant among the road specimens. A good habitat off the road may have as many as ten rabbits per acre, and an outstanding stretch of road may have three to four per mile (see world record in Chapter 1). During 1936 and 1937, the cottontail was the second most abundant mammal on Iowa's roadways, exceeded only by the thirteen-lined ground squirrel. The cars and trucks of the road habitat are just another predator in the life of a creature that seems almost designed to be killed and eaten. Young rabbits are produced in very large numbers and are especially obvious on the road in late spring and early summer when their lack of experience makes them particularly susceptible to all pred-ators. The cottontail is extremely fast over short distances and is able to cross a traffic lane in one or two exceedingly fast leaps. Unfortunately, it moves about mostly from dusk to dawn, and its usual first response to danger is to freeze and remain motionless. On the road, when the danger has passed, the cottontail is likely to remained permanently immobile.

4¹/₂ inches

Cottontail rabbit (*Sylvilagus* species)

The cottontail presents a clear and obvious denial of the superstition that a rabbit's foot brings good luck. Many of the road forms show at least three feet and no luck at all. Legs and ears are both easily visible in all of the usual presentations.

In general, it depends on lack of movement and protective coloration to save it; and neither works well on the road. Only approximately 10 percent of new rabbits survive the first year!

FIELD MARKS AND RANGE The name provides the most valuable single field mark. If you see a generally gray form of appropriate size with a white spot at one end and one or two three-inch ears visible at the other, it is most likely a cottontail. The various species found all across America are nearly identical in their road presentation. The Atlantic coastal forms are a bit darker and the Southwest desert species lighter, but the ears and tail are constant. The cottontail is a year-round road resident over all of its range, with the winter forms lasting much longer than the summer ones because of the cooler temperatures.

Armadillos (*Dasypus novemcinctus*)
17 x 12 inches, with a 15-inch tapered tail

HABITS AND ABUNDANCE The armadillo is near-sighted, has poorly developed hearing, and moves about mostly at night—a set of characteristics guaranteeing that relative to its numbers off the road, it will be better represented in the road fauna than any other mammal. Near-sightedness works well in locating the worms, grubs, and caterpillars that provide most of its food, but is of little help in helping the armadillo look both ways before crossing the highway. This creature also has a very fine sense of smell, but cars at 60 to 70 mph leave scent only behind them, never before. The armadillo is generally unaware that any vehicle is approaching until it is very near, and then the animal's startled response is to leap straight up into the air, usually to about bumper height. Armadillos can run with considerable speed, but they seldom make use of this skill on the road. A near miss by a passing pickup is likely to call forth the other response to disturbance—to curl up in a tight ball, with only the thickly plated back exposed. While this might puzzle a fox, it is no problem for an Audi. When severely hounded, the armadillos alternative response is to dig in—not useful on the interstate. This unaggressive, bumbling creature has few natural enemies except motorized vehicles.

FIELD MARKS AND RANGE The armadillo looks like nothing else on the road and is unlikely to be confused with any other similarly sized animal. Its appearance is more nearly the same before and after flattening than any other road creature. Unlike all other mammals in the guide, the armadillo has no extensive fur covering. It most closely resembles a small tank, with hinged armor plate covering the head, body, and tail. In a few cases, when severely flattened it might resemble a large turtle, but the presence of even a single ear will distinguish it from any shelled reptile. The ears may be three inches long.

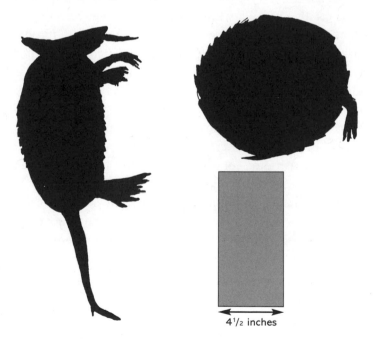

4¹/₂ inches

Armadillo (*Dasypus novemcinctus*)

An armadillo is one of those few creatures of any size that looks much the same on and off the road. The illustration on the right shows the curled, ineffective, protective presentation favored by some armadillos.

The armadillo has spread from Mexico since the 1850s, often helped along by travelers who carry them in cars for some distance.[9] They cannot survive any period of cold temperatures and will probably never be present anywhere north of southern Nebraska. Highways in rural parts of Texas and the Gulf Coast states are its preferred habitat.

Skunks (*Mephitis mephitis* and several related species)
20 x 12 inches, with a heavily furred 12-inch tail

HABITS AND ABUNDANCE This peaceable, gentle creature has refused to come to terms with highway traffic and continues to behave as if roads, cars, and trucks do not exist. Armed as it has always been with an odorous repellent strong enough to turn away any potential predator, it hops along totally unafraid, which is as fatal as overly aggressive behavior on the road. Its response to any threat is to turn its back and raise its tail in the air. The experienced predator retreats at this point, but cars generally behave with less intelligence. The skunk is not a hibernator, but it will sometimes den up with a few buddies during the colder months. It has been reported on the road during every month of the year; its occasional wintertime wanderings are most likely a response to spending too much time with a dozen sleeping skunks and sorely felt need for some fresh air. Most skunks are stay-at-homes; but during February and March, males scour the countryside every night for female companionship; and during late summer and autumn, juvenile males wander about looking for a place to spend the next few years.

FIELD MARKS AND RANGE Although olfactory clues are seldom significant in identifying road creatures, the skunk is a dramatic exception. It is obvious for miles along the road when a skunk is on its way to flat. When flattened into its

---

[9] There are documented examples of them showing up briefly far north of their usual range, being carried there in autos. Like turtles or small ducks, they are temporarily interesting, but make very poor pets.

permanent road form, there is seldom any odor, and some of the finest specimens will be missed if you come to depend on this single clue to its presence. The color pattern is unique, consisting of strongly contrasting black and white patches. The stripes may be longitudinal or sometimes spiral, if the skunk has been on the road for some time.

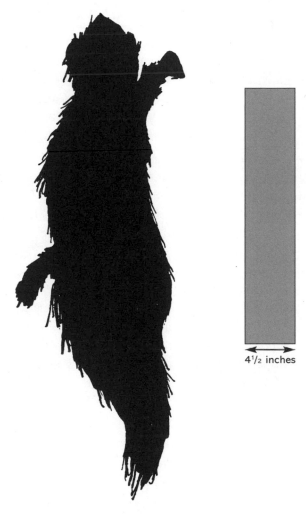

4¹/₂ inches

Skunk (*Mephitis mephitis*)

After a few days on the road, the skunk commonly assumes the position shown in this illustration.

The several species of skunk occur in every part of the U.S. and are more obvious on the road than any other creature. You never forget your first skunk, and even the fiftieth can be memorable.

Badgers (*Taxidea taxus*)
30 x 20 inches, with a 5-inch furry tail

The badger is the only North American mammal that at first glance looks as though it was designed for life on the road. It is flat, wide, and very low to the ground, vaguely resembling a miniature, multicolored sports car. Appearances are deceiving in this case: The badger is better designed for death than for life on the road.

HABITS AND ABUNDANCE Upon encountering a human, a badger will most often stand its ground for a few minutes, snarling and hissing. Upon encountering a car, a badger will usually behave the same way. Badgers are large and strong enough to fear little from most predators, but a Double Eagle (Goodyear) tire will get them every time. Digging is a daily activity for most badgers, as they move regularly over hundreds of acres, digging up the ground squirrels and other small animals that constitute their primary food. So much movement brings them onto the road frequently, and their aggressive nature often keeps them there permanently. When a badger genuinely wishes to escape from danger, its usual response is to dig in. Its powerful legs and long claws can put it below ground in seconds—unless, of course, it happens to be on a cement or asphalt surface, where such a survival response has little to recommend it.

FIELD MARKS AND RANGE All road badgers are flattened dorsi-ventrally. They are so nearly flat already that it is almost impossible for a badger to be on its side. The usual road specimen has mostly grizzled fur, with strong black and white markings at the pointed (head) end. The short tail is not prominent. This is the only road animal smaller than a bear with claws big enough to be seen at 50 mph. The digging claws at the front end of the animal are near the main part of the body and are nearly as long as the legs. Its legs are short and are located at each corner of the basically rectangular shape.

The badger is present on roads from the Great Lakes region to the West Coast, and from Canada to Mexico. It is one of the most abundant carnivores on the road, exceeded in number only by rabbits, raccoons, skunks, muskrats, and opossums.

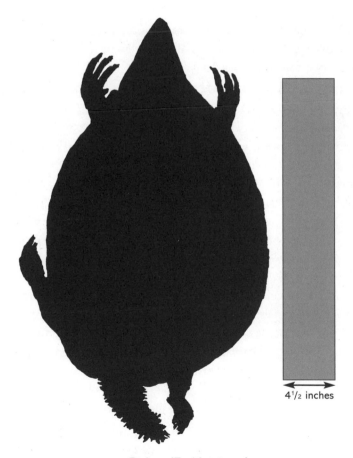

4¹/₂ inches

Badger (*Taxidea taxus*)

The badger is the largest, flattest creature to be found on the road. Some are larger and some may be flatter, but nowhere else are those two characteristics so combined.

Jackrabbits, Antelope Hares, Snowshoe Hares
(*Lepus californicus* [black] or *Lepus townsendii* [white tail], *Lepus alleni*, *Lepus americanus*)
24 inches x 6–8 inches

These large hares are abundant and active year-round over most of the western U.S. In warmer climates the legs and ears are both noticeably longer than in the more northerly parts of their range. At times these animals will have the highest population density of any road mammal, with hundreds of flat rabbits scattered along a few miles of two-lane road. (See record on page 3.)

HABITS AND ABUNDANCE Although they may live for many years in captivity, in the vicinity of roads (i.e., almost anywhere in the U.S.), 60 to 90 percent of juvenile hares survive less than a year. The young are precocial and can run, feed, and die independently of adults almost from the moment of birth. They appear to receive little parental instruction on the hazards of the road and most often freeze into immobility when frightened. The lights of a car or truck will often fix a jackrabbit to its place on the road even before the wheel arrives to put its permanent stamp on the location. Older hares are in less danger, since they are likely to run, and can achieve speeds of up to 35 mph. Even adults sometimes overestimate their capacity to avoid danger, however, and find themselves half an inch high and roughly rectangular. Jackrabbits often use exactly the same trails repeatedly, and the same highway location will often sport several hares in succession if the traffic lane bisects the rabbit lane. Death in the fast lane is a way of life for many rabbits.

FIELD MARKS AND RANGE At least one of the large ears (up to eight inches long) will usually show in almost any road presentation. An object of a generally grayish or brownish hue, with what appears to be more than four appendages, is almost surely a jackrabbit or a near relative. Being larger than most of the road fauna and not at all compact in shape, the road jackrabbit has a greater tendency to spread out, disconnect, and scatter its parts than many of its smaller and more nearly square companions. The southwestern species are particularly likely to be found in several lanes at the same time, partly the result of their speed and partly the result of the speed of traffic.

Nearly every state west of the Mississippi River has jackrabbits, and nearly any stretch of road in open country will harbor a few year-round. These are never found in cities, except occasionally in the outer reaches of Los Angeles.

4^1/$_2$ inches

Jackrabbit (*Lepus* species)

The illustration is meant to convey the form of a jackrabbit that has kept itself together, more or less. Commonly, jackrabbits will be separated and spread out somewhat. Part of the animal may be presented laterally, and part dorsi-ventrally.

Porcupines (*Orethizon dorsatum*)

20 x 14 inches with a 10-inch long-haired tail

HABITS AND ABUNDANCE The porcupine generally lives out its eight to ten years in peaceful solitude, bumbling along from tree to tree, crossing the road only to get to the other pine. While porcupines are not what could be called agile climbers, they do spend a lot of time in tree tops feeding on bark. On the ground they are clumsy at best and at worst seem to have little idea where they are headed. As is characteristic of animals that do not feel threatened by most predators, they have relatively poor eyesight. A car at a distance of more than fifty feet is probably not recognizable to even an auto-wise porcupine. They have good hearing and respond readily to nearly all sounds but that of an auto horn. Their reaction to a threat is to erect the sharp quills that cover the back and tail, and to flail the air with the tail. Such an act will deter even the hungriest wolf or wildcat, but does not slow down a Mustang or Jaguar. (Quills can, and should, be removed from tires with a pair of pliers. If left in place they will work their way to the heart of the radial and may cause serious deflation.) The young porcupines are independent of their mother after only a few weeks and are most likely to be found on the road at that time. They do not hibernate and may become part of the road fauna in any season.

FIELD MARKS AND RANGE The porcupine is the largest animal that can be flattened on most road surfaces. A mature adult may weigh up to thirty pounds, but most of the road specimens will be the young of that year and only half that size. The hair is extremely long, longer than the quills, and the animal may seem larger than the dimensions given. Individual hairs may be eight inches long, and their light-colored tips and darker roots may give the animal a grizzled appearance. Often a specimen will mimic a clump of dirt with dark straw extending out in all directions.

Coniferous forests are the preferred habitat, but the range extends into the grasslands of Nebraska. Porcupines are found over most of North America except for the southeast and south-central parts of the U.S.

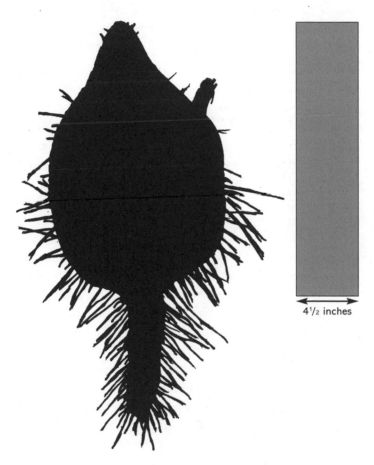

4¹/₂ inches

Porcupine (*Orethizon dorsatum*)

It makes little difference how a porcupine is initially arrayed on the road; it quickly assumes a nearly square silhouette, with the legs barely visible. The bristles and tail identify it regardless of orientation.

Raccoons (*Procyon lotor*)
20–30 inches x 12–16 inches with
an 8–10-inch, striped, bushy tail

Because of the black mask on a usually whitish face, the rac-coon looks something like a bandit (highwayman would be a more appropriate nickname). Raccoons are almost always equal to skunks in the number found on the road.

HABITS AND ABUNDANCE Curiosity is a dominant trait in both the young and the adult raccoon. It is the sort of impulse that might cause a raccoon to stop and stare at a new model of car on the road, thus producing most of the adult flat raccoons. The breeding season is long, and males travel extensively in search of receptive females from Janu-ary to almost June. Any mostly nocturnal animal is likely to respond inappropriately to sudden light, because until the twentieth century night was not interrupted by anything more dangerous than lightning. And since most raccoons travel at night (before midnight), they are frequently on the road for several days thereafter. The young of the year (from two to five per litter) begin nocturnal traveling and feeding with mom about August. They often follow in a line behind her, with the smallest trailing at the end of the line. The last in line is most often the first to be flattened on the road, and many of the road raccoons are the small, slow tail-enders.

FIELD MARKS AND RANGE The five to seven dark rings on the bushy tail are the most reliable and durable single road feature. The black facial mask is only visible in some orien-tations, but if there are patches of black at the opposite end from the striped tail, you are surely looking at a raccoon. Larger raccoons, which may weigh up to sixty pounds, are too large to flatten even on the busiest roads. Only rarely will any animal that large develop a recognizable silhouette. The illustrations on the following page are suggestive rather than descriptive. During late fall and early winter, when the pelt is at its greatest thickness and toughness, even some of the largest road raccoons will develop the characteristic teardrop form, with black patterning at the pointed end and the striped tail at the other.[10]

Raccoons occur throughout the U.S., southern Canada, and Mexico. They are rare to absent in the higher altitudes of the mountainous West.

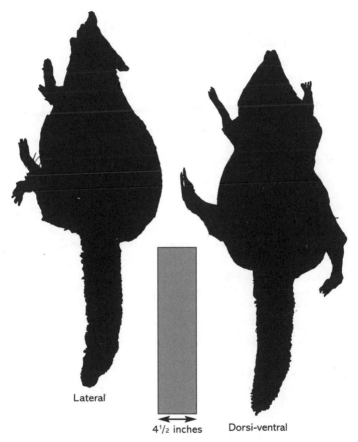

Lateral

4¹/₂ inches   Dorsi-ventral

Raccoon (*Procyon lotor*)

Raccoons are a little too thick toward the tail to flatten well. The illustrations presented here are a bit more like vertical projections of what is found on the road. A two-dimensional raccoon is truly rare. Even after most of the raccoon has disappeared from the road, the remaining tail will be a persistent reminder of where the animal was.

---

10 If you see what appears to be a small raccoon with a tail at least as long as its body, and if you are in Texas or the Southwest, you are looking at a ringtail (*Bassariscus astutus*), a near relative of the raccoon with similar habits.

Bibliography

Adams, Clark E. 1983. Road-killed animals as resources for ecological studies. *The American Biology Teacher* 45:256–261.

Aaris-Sorensen, J. 1995. Road-kills of badgers in Denmark. *Ann. Sool. Fennici* 32:31–36.

Behler, John L. 1995. *National Audubon Society Field Guide to North American Reptiles and Amphibians*. New York: Alfred A. Knopf.

Bent, Arthur Cleveland. Life histories of American birds. *Bulletins of the United States National Museum*. (The Bent Life Histories of American Birds are in a large number of volumes. They are sequentially numbered and each deals with a specific group of birds.)

Butz, Bob. 2005. *Beast of Never, Cat of God: The Search for the Eastern Puma*. Guilford, CT: Lyons Press.

Chapman, J. A. and G. A. Feldhamer, eds. 1982. *Wild Animals of North America*. Baltimore: Johns Hopkins University Press.

Drews, C. 1995. Road-kills of animals by public traffic in Mikumi National Park, Tanzania. *African Journal of Ecology*, 33:89–100.

Garland, Theodore, Jr. and W. Glen Bradley. 1984. Effects of a highway on Mohave Desert rodent populations. *American Midland Naturalist* 111:47–56.

Jones, J. Knox, Jr., D. M. Armstrong, R. S. Hoffman, and C. Jones. 1983. *Mammals of the Northern Great Plains*. Lincoln: University of Nebraska Press.

McClure, H. Elliot. 1951. An analysis of animal victims on Nebraska's highways. *Journal of Wildlife Management* 15:410–420.

Monge-Najera, J. 1996. Vertebrate mortality on tropical highways: the Costa Rican case. *Vide Silvestre Neotropical* 5:154–156.

Peterson, Roger Tory. 1947. *A Field Guide to the Birds*. Boston: Houghton Mifflin.

Robbins, C. S., Bruun Bertel, and H. S. Zim. 1966. *Birds of North America*. New York: Bolden Press.

Scott, Thomas G. 1938. Wildlife mortality on Iowa highways. *American Midland Naturalist* 20:527–539.

Sheffer, Victor B. 1983. *Spires of Form, Glimpses of Evolution*. Seattle: University of Washington Press.

Simmons, James R. 1983. *Feathers and Fur on the Turnpike*. Boston: Christopher Publishing House.

Yom-Tov, Yoram. 1997. The evolution of two-dimensional vertebrates. *Israel Journal of Zoology* 43:217–218.

Index